The

Broken

Vase

Written By
Durmond L. Glanton

Published By: Tamika INK

Library of Congress Cataloging – in- Publication Data has been applied for.

ISBN: 979-8-9854737-7-3

PRINTED IN THE UNITED STATES OF AMERICA.

Dedication

I'd like to dedicate this book in Loving memory of my Father, Thurman Harrell Sr.

Pop, not a day goes by that I don't miss you. Thank you for being the prime example of what it is to be a man, father, husband, son, and an all-around great human soul. Hope I've made you proud. This one's for you, Pop.

Table of Contents

Chapter One

This is a story about a vase, a vase that was given as a gift to a special young man as a wedding gift. This vase was great in value, not because of its cost, but because of who had gifted it. When given the vase, this young man made a vow to himself to cherish the vessel and never allow it to lose its value.

Five years later, one fateful day, this vow would be broken. As the young man played with his two-year-old daughter, chasing her around the house and rolling on the living room floor with her, the thunderous laughs and beautiful bonding between a father and his daughter came to a crushing end when they bumped into the coffee table, causing the valued vase to fall to the floor. The vase shattered into multiple pieces. Like the broken vase, the man's heart was also shattered into pieces. How could he let this happen? The inner questions flooded his mind as he stared at the shattered pieces in disappointment. "What am I going to do? How can I explain this to her?" he asked himself.

With his toddler on his hip, overwhelmed with sadness and disappointment, the blank stare continued, accompanied by dead silence. Suddenly, out of the depths of his empty thoughts, a revelation enlightened him, which resurrected his excitement and energy. So, I guess THIS is where the REAL STORY begins.

My story began on Thursday, July 14, 1977; a miracle baby boy named Durmond Lavell Glanton was introduced to the world, only weighing 4 pounds 2 ounces. However, since the announcement of my arrival, the devil had plots and schemes to eliminate me. At the age of 6 months old, the first attempt on my life was halted. My mother and her best friend pulled up to the house with groceries. Talking, laughing, and having fun, doing what best friends do, I'm sure. While getting the rest of the groceries from the trunk of the car, my mother's best friend thought the coast was clear. She closed the trunk, slamming it directly on the back of my neck. I don't remember this incident, but my mom informed me years later of it, and when it happened, she thought my neck was instantly broken. They both frantically rushed me to the emergency room, and after being checked by the doctor, it was determined that my neck was only badly bruised, *not* broken and that I would be just fine. **MISSION FAILED**.

By the age of four, I fell in love with my first musical instrument of interest, the drums. The sound of the cymbals, the boom of the toms and bass drum, and the vibe and movements of the rhythm it brought captivated my heart, mind, and soul. During this time of my life, my mother was still living at my grandparents' home in a small town in upstate New York called Williamson. During this time of my life, my mother was back and forth from New York to Florida, working on saving her marriage with my biological father, who wasn't a part of my life. I was raised by and lived with my grandparents as a toddler.

My family was large, but we were very poor. I remember on many occasions looking out of the window of what our family deemed "The Green House" and seeing my grandfather walking home from work. I would later find out that he walked approximately two miles each way to and from work, even in the freezing cold or the blistering heat.

My grandmother would ensure his plate of food was hot and ready for him whenever he got home. I would sit and watch him refuse to eat his food until he knew all his children, grandchildren, and even a few neighborhood children had eaten supper and were full. That's the type of man he was. There would be times that I witnessed him scraping scraps from other plates to accumulate a meal of his own. *"Rest In Peace" Mr. Clyde Neil Sr., my granddad.*

I remember one Saturday morning, he was sitting in the living room playing his guitar. I'm not sure what he was playing, but I found the rhythm even at the age of four; I started making beats on the couch, tables, and walls. At that moment, he recognized something great within me and knew I was destined for greatness. But there was a slight problem; although he saw I was great with rhythm, he couldn't afford to buy me a drum set to help push that gift out of me. But when you're determined, you're *determined.* He would often cut two limbs from a tree in his backyard, turnover a couple of pots and pans on the kitchen floor, sit me in the middle of them, and allow me to play my heart out. In those moments, I took to the rhythm I knew and taught myself how to play the drums. Once my grandfather told my mother of my gift, she would take my brothers and me to a church she attended down the street. We would attend every Sunday and a few days during the week whenever she was in town.

There was a pretty white drum set at the church, and even though there were plenty of drummers there, I would practice on that drum set every chance I could get. By the time I was six years old, me, my oldest brother Shaft, and our Uncle Anthony were the church drummers, and I was very skilled at it. Many spectators from visiting churches were amazed at this "little boy's" drumming skills at such a young age. For that reason alone, I remained faithful as a drummer at Redeem COGIC.

Chapter Two

B y the age of 8, in 1985, I experienced my first true heartbreak; I remember it like it was yesterday. In March, on that Monday afternoon, I was waiting in the bus loop with my older brothers, Shaft and Johnnie, and some other friends from the neighborhood, including Shaft's best friend, Chad. We all lived in the same apartment/townhouse complex nearby. We always played football, baseball, and tag; we would breakdance in the open field that was in the complex. Sometimes, we would play basketball at a nearby court, where the community's older teens and young adults would spend most of their time playing.

While on the bus headed home, I remember my brother and Chad making plans to get together and play baseball with some more of the neighborhood kids. I *never* really got the chance to hang out with Shaft and his friends much because of the age difference. On the other hand, Johnnie was closer in age, so he was able to hang out and play with them in most cases.

I remember pleading with them, "Can I play? Please? I never get to play with you guys." Even though I wanted to play football with them, and baseball was what they wanted to play, it didn't matter; I just wanted to be a part of it.

"Yea, man, you can play," my oldest brother, Shaft, assured me, and I was so excited. Shaft and Chad were the most popular kids in that age group and probably in the entire complex, now that I think about it. Yes, to be able to play ball with them was a massive win for me being a kid that looked up to them both.

While getting off the bus, we said, "Goodbye and see ya later," and rushed home to do our chores and homework so that we could leave and meet up to play some baseball with Chad and some friends.

However, when we got to the house, my mother had different plans for us. As we walked through the door, she said, "Alright, Y'all do your schoolwork, shower, I'm gonna cook, we're going to eat, then y'all gotta get dressed because we're going to church tonight." What! CHURCH, on a Monday?

I remember Shaft begging my mother, "Ma, we wanted to go play baseball with Chad! We always do. Can we just stay home?"

But Momma would not budge. She repeatedly told us, "No, we're going to church; y'all can play with Chad anytime." I mean, go figure. The ONE TIME I got to hang with my brothers and his friends, I couldn't. Why? Because I had to go to church!

We went to one of our bedrooms and had straight attitudes, as you can imagine. We weren't too fond of the church because momma made it a point for us to be with her regularly. So, as we sat in the room and complained, I, along with my brothers, heard a sound ring out throughout the complex that sounded like a huge firecracker went off. We kind of brushed it off with the anger we felt about not being able to play.

As an eight-year-old kid, I despised the fact that I was so sheltered, mainly because of the church. I couldn't go to a friend's house nor spend the night there. No movies, breakdancing, bike riding, fort building, all the stuff little boys did. I really couldn't because the church was a priority. So as the time went by, about an hour and a half from us getting home from school, we were still sitting in my brother's room, salty and upset, when the phone rang.

We didn't really hear my mom answer, but suddenly, we heard her screaming, "WHAT'S THE MATTER? WHAT HAPPENED?"

As momma continued to scream, we all jumped up and sprinted downstairs to come to her aid. As we're racing downstairs, I hear my mom say, "Ok, I'm on my way up there!" She frantically told us to get in the car because something was going on at the top of the complex. My brothers nor I knew what was going on, but we sensed something was wrong. We pulled up to the 1000 block of the complex. We couldn't even pull into the parking lot because police cars, fire trucks, ambulances, and rescue trucks were everywhere. They were parked awkwardly, all with the red and blue lights flashing. So now we knew something was wrong.

We all jumped out of the car, and my mom sprinted towards apartment 1001, Chad's house, with me and my brothers trailing behind her. All I can remember was hearing the screams of horror and the sounds of crying as outside onlookers cried and embraced each other. Still not knowing what happened, my mom opened the door and was stopped by an officer, a black man dressed in a suit, "Ma'am, you can't go in there," as she tried to make her way in to see what was going on.

As my mother explained to the officer that we were like family (again, I remember it like it was yesterday), the officer said to my mom, "Ok, listen, ma'am, Chad has been shot."

I'll never forget the sharp pain that hit my chest as I saw my mother hit the ground in tears. Me and my brothers then ran outside and saw all the neighborhood kids crying with local police officers, along with New York State troopers consoling and comforting all of the children who knew Chad.

We didn't know how serious the situation was, but we knew Chad was harmed, bringing a gloomy dark cloud over the entire complex. So, we all sat outside and waited. Let me just say this; it was the most extended wait of my life. Anxieties and impatience flooded the air as we all sat and waited to see how badly our friend was injured. Our hearts paced, and our minds wandered as we saw numerous cops go in and out of our friend's place. Then in an instant, I saw the same officer who initially stopped my mom from going into Chad's house, leaving the scene where the incident happened, and walking back towards apartment 1001. He had an entourage behind him in suits and uniforms. At that moment, we knew he had some more information about our friend. So, we all followed them back to Chad's to get the same details that everyone else was getting.

The apartment was crowded; there were family members and friends everywhere. The officers walked in to see a pillar of the community, who we all knew as "Miss Mamie," Chad's mom. I saw the pain in her eyes as she sat on the couch, being held and surrounded by family. I remember the officer telling her, " I'm sorry, we did all that we could to save him, but Chad just passed."

I literally felt my heart crumble into pieces at that very moment as the screams exploded throughout the house and the outside surrounding areas. My friend was gone at the age of 11!

Did it mean no more football? No more baseball? No more tag, and no more basketball and breakdancing? How could *any* of these activities take place without Chad? It didn't seem real. Chad was the most influential friend I ever had. He was close with my oldest brother but close to everyone who knew him. He had the best smile, the greatest laugh, and the funniest jokes. He was just the coolest kid in the neighborhood, and I was a part of his circle. I was blessed to be in his world.

He taught me how to throw a football with a tight spiral; he was also the first person to teach me how to dribble a basketball between my legs without any fumbles. As kids, we all knew that Chad would grow up and do big and great things in life, but that all came to a crashing halt as we all saw the medical examiner push a lifeless body bag on top of a stretcher into the back of the van. We screamed, we hollered, and we cried in disbelief because we knew that inside of that body bag was the body of our friend we loved so much. I didn't sleep much that night; I spent most of the night crying, tossing, and turning.

As an eight-year-old kid, I thought, "Man, we were just laughing and playing with him yesterday. We just saw him today at school, and we were supposed to have played baseball. How could this happen?"

Shaft was more hurt than all of us. This was his best friend. I mean, they were so close; they even called each other "cousins," knowing they weren't related. Although our uncle was married to his sister at the time, that was our way of solidifying ourselves as family. It doesn't get much closer than that! Shaft was never the same after we lost Chad. School wasn't the same either; the halls were quiet, it seemed like there was no energy, and the school flag that was visible from most classrooms hung halfway down the pole. The neighborhood atmosphere wasn't the same either. No pickup games, no loud music blasting, no kids running around, and no bike riding. There was a cloud of silence and heartbreak throughout the complex. We had truly lost a young legend in our community.

There are many theories and stories about how we lost Chad. So many have great memories and stories to tell about Chad. Whatever the case may be, SO MANY remembered how he died; I REMEMBERED HOW HE LIVED! He was an Angel on earth. Let me take this moment to send special love to Miss Mamie, Earl, Webster, Chuck, Janice, Delores, Cassandra, and the entire Blackmon family. The **#Chad11** legacy will never die. Rest In Paradise, the kid, the legend, Chad Eugene Blackmon.

Chapter Three

The second attempt on my life happened when I was eight years old. By this time, my mother was back in New York full time, divorced, and living in her own apartment with me and my older brothers in a town called "Webster." I was standing at the bus stop waiting to go to school in the freezing cold. It was snowing hard, and I remember it piling up so ridiculously. I was bundled up and wrapped up from head to toe like a mummy. I remember quite a few kids being at the bus stop along with my brothers. That's when a car came speeding around the curve and hit an ice patch which caused it to spin out of control, heading straight for the bus stop where we all were standing.

I remembered being strapped to the gurney and being asked NOT to move. I had been hit by a car, which briefly knocked me unconscious. My mom was called at work and was informed as to what just happened to me and left work to head straight to the hospital. I was immediately rushed to the hospital via ambulance.

"it's ok, buddy, you're gonna be ok," I heard from the EMTs as tears fell down my face from fear. They continued to talk and comfort me all the way to the hospital.

Once I was taken into a room, I remember seeing the doctors and nurses inspecting my body, checking for broken bones and bruises. Before I knew it, my mother came into the room while the medical team was still working and started laying hands on me, pleading the blood of Jesus Christ over my body. After a thorough check-up on me, my mother was told by the doctor that I had no broken bones, no bumps or bruises, and the snowbank that I landed in *head first* was the reason for no serious head injuries. **MISSION FAILED.**

So, you may ask, "Durmond, is this really your story, sir?"

No, not at all. These are early testimonies as reminders that the Devil ALWAYS had a PLOT, but God ALWAYS had a PLAN! I could really keep going on with testimonies of my life as a young child, and a preteen, and I promise when

I have the time, I will share them with you all; however, let me get back to the story.

I have served as a musician at church ever since I can remember. I had a serious passion for playing the drums. I dedicated myself to every service, whether Sunday morning, Sunday afternoon program, Sunday evening, choir rehearsal, Friday night service, revival, or conference. Even as a child, I would perfect my gift as a drummer every chance I got to play. Of course, there are always challenging oppositions, even with hard work and dedication. Even after the Lord saved me and filled me with The Holy Ghost, I dealt with serious spiritual warfare. I'm sure that many can attest to this.

When I first got saved, man, I was on fire for God for real. I attended every service, every Bible study, read my word every day, paid tithes and offering, and despite the critics giving me a timeframe saying, "He'll be back in the world in no time," I was determined to live right and serve God until I had nothing left. That was my vow to Him; after all, He saved me from a life of sin, right?

I was 19 years old, a few months from turning 20; I was only saved a few months, still a faithful drummer at the church. My best friend, Matt, who is also my godbrother, was the church organist and man, let me tell you, he was amazing! He is still a fantastic organist to this day, but he wasn't saved at the time. A situation came about in his life where our pastor, who happened to be his father, sat him down from playing the organ on Sunday mornings and all services at the church.

The church seemed to be in a tough spot now; where would we find another organist of his caliber to perform during the service on Sunday mornings and throughout the week? I heard God's actual voice for the first time during those moments. He spoke to me and said, "You do it!"

Now, remember, I was still a drummer during these times, but the church had another drummer besides me who also played on some Sundays, mostly during our weekly services. I remember thinking, "Me, God? I'm not an organist, I'm a drummer, but I'll do it."

Growing up in the church my whole life, I've been taught consistently that **to obey is better than sacrifice.** I never really understood it; I didn't understand why people in church said it often. In fact, I used to get sick of hearing it. However, when it becomes personal and applies to **YOU,** you will understand why it's important to obey God when He instructs us. So, I told the Lord, "Lord, if you anoint me for it, I will try."

The first couple of Sundays playing as a "replacement" organist was very tough. I felt so embarrassed as I tried to put chords together to carry the same service that my godbrother did smoothly and efficiently. However, I struggled to find keys and follow my Godfather as he preached so hard. Although the congregation fought through it and bared with me and my musical mistakes, I played with my head down, knowing I was failing the service, and most importantly, I thought I was failing God Himself.

I remember calling Matt discouraged. I told him, "Bro, I don't know if I can do this. It's harder than I imagined." His response to me was the first actual step in me learning to be an effective musician in church.

He said, "Durmond, that's because you're trying to play like *me*. You're trying to carry the service as I would, and you're even trying to sound the way I sound. You have to be yourself."

At that moment, God dealt with me spiritually, reminding me that when David was preparing to conquer the giant **(1 Samuel:17)**, Saul equipped David with his armor to wear. However, the armor didn't fit, making David uncomfortable because, truthfully, David didn't fight the way Saul fought. David may have very well put on Saul's armor and went out to battle, but in retrospect, would he have been as effective using armor that worked for someone else? So how did David deal with this situation without offending his leader? He remembered his prior victories by remembering that God has always equipped him for the task at hand. We must know that no matter the battle, no matter how big the giant is, we always **overcome by the blood of the lamb and by the words of our testimony.** So, David was victorious by using what worked for him. So, I began to pray daily and ask God to equip me for this tedious task.

My mother, who was at the time and still is an international evangelist began to anoint my hands daily and pray *the Prayer of Faith* for God to anoint my hands and stir up the gifts that were already in me. The more I practiced during the week in her basement, the better I became, and before you know it, within a month's time, I was able to play more smoothly and effectively, carrying a service using and creating my own sound.

I still can't remember the exact moment when I was able to play with confidence during a service for the first time. However, I do know that God equipped me for it, and it was my "Yes" to Him that brought this gift about. THANK YOU, JESUS!!!

By the age of 23, I played the organ/keys at church alongside my godbrother, falling more and more in love with music as I grew as a minstrel. Still saved, sanctified, and filled with the Holy Ghost, I was on fire for God, married, and just enjoying life as a Christian man. Here's where my life began to really change. Why? I received the call from God to preach the gospel of Jesus Christ. I knew it was the Lord who called me because it was the same voice who told me to step out on faith and become an organist. That alone gave me the confidence to do it. Not to mention, I was trying so hard to labor in the church, not only as a musician but walking beside my Godfather as a preacher? Yes! I just wanted to please God. I had the support of my mother, my father, my brothers, the rest of my family, and the saints at the church.

So again, I told the Lord "Yes," and did what was necessary to transition from a musician to minister on the ministerial staff at the church.

Whenever I was called upon to minister, I gave it all I had. I knew I wasn't just a "Preacher," but God anointed me *to preach*. There's a vast difference between being a preacher and being anointed by God to preach. Because I was anointed to preach, it didn't take long for God to call me into evangelism. Yes, it was a great task, but again I gave God a "Yes" and started traveling to various churches locally and around the country to preach the gospel. I preached at conferences, and revivals, from city to city and state to state. I was serving the Lord, serving my Godfather as a faithful minister at my home church, being a husband, and serving other ministries on the road as an Evangelist. LIFE WAS GOOD. I was happy and on top of the world. Nothing could possibly shake my faith, right?

Chapter Four

Well, I experienced another devastating heartbreak and serious spiritual warfare as an adult in July of 2004. I was considered a "seasoned" preacher by this time. I was still saved, filled with the Holy Ghost, and on fire. It was literally two days before my 27th birthday. I was excited that God blessed me to see another year. I was happy, still married, a father to a beautiful baby girl, still traveling and preaching, and I was established in God (so I thought). I was also enjoying the tail end of my family reunion in my hometown. Enjoying the fellowship with my cousins, aunts, uncles, grandparents, etc., lots of laughs, singing, music, praying, tears, and good eating, you name it, my family experienced it during the family reunion.

On Monday, July 12, 2004, most of my family was heading back to their homes out of state; the reunion had ended.

It was Dad's birthday, and I wanted to stay with him and my mom to celebrate while my wife, at the time, went to play cards with my aunts at another location. Where was the baby, you may ask? She was in the Intensive Care Unit at the local hospital suffering from pneumonia due to some complications from birth. As parents, we spent all our time staying overnight at the hospital with our daughter, Iyana. My mother thought it was a good idea for us to get our minds off the stress of the hospital for a couple of days and just enjoy family while they were in town for the reunion. So, I planned to chill with my dad for an hour or two for his birthday, then head up to the hospital to check on "YaYa" and stay the night at the hospital with her.

As I was getting ready to leave my parent's house to head up to the hospital, my phone rang. As I looked at the screen, I could see the hospital calling. I thought, "Yea, they're probably calling to see what time we're coming up there, so the nurse on the floor can be on watch for us."

I'll never forget this phone call. My mother followed me into the room as I calmly answered the phone. It's almost like she knew something was going to be wrong. "Hello," I answered, and that's when the concerned voice on the other end of the phone said, *"Hello, Mr. Glanton? This is the nurse calling from ICU; we ran into a problem about 10 minutes ago, Iyana has coded for the second time today, and we are currently trying to resuscitate her."*

I didn't even let her finish talking, nor did I reply to her. I threw my phone down and started to cry as my mother saw my facial expression and knew there was a problem with her granddaughter. She grabbed me and said, "Ok, son, get yourself together, let's go; I'll drive."

She informed my dad what was happening, and we headed out the door with him following behind us in his truck, heading for the hospital. My mother called my aunts to inform my wife that there was a problem at the hospital.

The entire ride there, I reminded God of my faithfulness to him and that I needed Him to show up for me like He had every time before. As I began to weep, I was also speaking into the atmosphere that everything would be ok. Here I am, a Man of God, faithful not only to God but also to my marriage, faithful at my church; truly, God will honor me and my request to Him, right? My mom dropped me off at the hospital's front door while she parked, and I remember sprinting through the hospital, trying to make it to the pediatric floor. I don't even think I used the elevator but instead hit the staircase, trying to get there to my baby's room as fast as possible.

When I got to the floor, I was met by my Aunt Linda, who tried to slow me down from getting to the room. "Durmond, wait a sec, baby!" she said as she held her arms out to stop me from getting past her.

Well, that didn't work as I brushed past my aunt with ease, heading towards Iyana's room. As I got to the room's door, I heard doctors and nurses conversing as I pulled back the curtain to enter the room. What I saw was enough to break any loving father's heart. I saw doctors pumping my daughter's chest, trying to revive her.

I yelled, "What's going on here?" as I saw my baby's limp body thrust on the table and flatlines on the monitors.

One of the doctors, probably not knowing I was the baby's father, turned around and screamed back at me, " YOU, GET THE H**L OUT OF HERE!" pointing towards the door with anger.

If I can just be honest with you all at this moment, I literally snapped at the entire staff. I started to lunge at them with bad intentions. After all, that was my daughter on the table.

At the time, I wasn't sure who it was, but I was lifted and carried out of the room despite being angry. I later found out it was my aunt Linda who carried me out of the room, and I'll never figure out how she did it, but I thank God she did. I sat in the waiting room as the family started to pour in for support. My anger began to dissipate as some family members told jokes to make me smile. We all stood together hand in hand, and Momma rendered a family prayer, pleading for the Lord's Will to be done. I had the faith; I really believed that God would show Himself mighty in this situation by raising YaYa and allowing her to live with every ounce of my being.

The doctors, two males, and one female entered the waiting room. They asked to speak to only me and my wife in private. We went into a private room; they began explaining what was happening with Iyana to cause the emergency codes. I saw the doctor who I had snapped at initially, and I apologized to him for my actions and asked him for forgiveness. We shook hands, and everything was fine from that point on.

The doctor explained that she had a severe coughing spell that caused her to aspirate, which caused her lungs to fill with liquid, requiring the code and need for resuscitation.

Naturally, being who I was, I asked, "So, she's ok then, right?"

That's when the other doctor took the conversation and began to tell us that they were able to bring back a pulse, and they were able to get her to breathe with the assistance of a machine, but there was no brain activity. *Wait, but I'm a man of God; I know He can fix this, so I was completely optimistic, thinking, "Ok, where there's a will, there's a way. Now God, MAKE A WAY!"*

When my wife asked the doctors, "Are you saying that our daughter is brain dead?"

Their response was given by simply nodding their heads "yes," with a look of grief on their faces. I'll never forget the feeling I had at that moment, as though my heart was dancing in the back of my throat. We had a decision to make; do we take her off the machine and let her die or give her a fighting chance at life, although statistically, she wouldn't survive? I mean, she was only two years old.

After we consulted the doctor for recommendations, we made the heartbreaking decision as her parents to let her be with Jesus. Just as any dad, I cried my eyes out along with my wife. I remembered the doctors, right in that private room, began to hug us and thank us for allowing them to care for Iyana. You would think that would make me feel better, right? It didn't. I had to go and tell the family that we were letting her go. We all cried together, and I remember my dad held me and cried with me, which was the first and ONLY time I saw him cry myself.

Now for the most challenging part of the entire day. We all went into Iyana's room, watched the doctors unplug the machines, and held her as she took her last breaths.

As a father, I can't even begin to express the internal pain I felt. This was my baby girl, my miracle child, my pride and joy, along with Imani, her older sister; why on earth would God take her from me? I reminded God I had been faithful, "I walked upright before you; I've been preaching your word wherever you sent me. God, you told me that you would come through for me if I only believed. I had the faith that you would Show yourself mighty in this. WHY GOD, Just WHY?"

These were the internal questions I asked as my sadness turned into anger. The pain of holding your baby as she takes her last breath isn't something I would wish on my worst enemy. But I had to be calm, cool, and collected. I couldn't allow anyone to see me break; my strength gives others strength.

"Just be cool, D. don't let it break you," I told myself. Although I was overwhelmingly sad and angry, I kept the brokenness **inside** and kept a smile on my face in front of everyone as we prepared to bury my child.

Throughout the week leading up to her services, I remember keeping the feelings I felt inside, especially in front of family, friends, and church family, which is literally everybody. Because I'm known now as a humble, cool, quiet, passive, and non-confrontational preacher, I couldn't get out of character. *Nobody* could see the cracks of brokenness on the inside, and to be honest, I refused to let anyone see me break.

Even at her funeral, I was all smiles, handshakes, and hugs, greeting those who showed up to support. Even when the funeral home workers lowered her toddler-sized casket to the ground, I felt the pain, but I disciplined myself to be "cool." Not because I was cool, but because no one could see the cracks of brokenness inside me if I continued to *display* strength.

So, there I was, *broken* on the inside, cool on the outside, and NOT completely healed and delivered.

Chapter Five

F ast forward to the Spring of 2008. Life was a little different now; I was still saved, filled with the Holy Ghost, and preaching the gospel. I was still married and now the father of two beautiful babies, a two-year-old girl and a five-month-old son. I was still serving God with all my might, and I was hanging on to Him with every bit of salvation in me.

Rumors surfaced, bad things had been said about me, and now my name was tainted. And you know what? It hurt. It hurt like you wouldn't believe; you know why? Because it wasn't coming from people I didn't know, it was coming from some of the ones I'd fellowshipped with every week at church. It came from those I thought genuinely cared about me, who knew I was in God and respected my character. I never imagined going through *this*. No, no way. Not in the church.

Nevertheless, I was determined to serve God wholeheartedly, so there I was again, cracked and *broken* on the inside. I was not dealing with or confronting my issues; while displaying strength and calmness on the outside, yet not healed and not delivered. I may have seemed cool, but inside I was utterly stressed, bleeding to death; I really cared about what people thought about me.

"Swift to hear, slow to speak, Durmond," I would tell myself. So, I would smile the hurt away, remain humble, and focus on preaching the gospel. The more lies I heard, the harder I preached. And you know what? It worked, but only on the outside. The stress was starting to take a toll on me as a husband. Now note this, I can only speak of my marriage from *my* perspective. I am not here to belittle nor slander my ex-wife because truth be told, I wasn't the perfect husband. I just need to tell it how I saw it back then.

I was working nearly 70 to 80 hours a week. Not only that, but I didn't have a reliable vehicle at the time, so I walked about 3½ miles to and from work each way. My wife was not working at the time. She had issues with kidney stones and hadn't worked consistently since

2002 when Iyana was born. So, there was literally one income in the house to pay all the bills. As a father and husband, I felt like I was doing it all alone, and it was very frustrating – dealing with small children and a wife who was borderline sickly. The sense of feeling alone and Yet, between the stress and turmoil, I remained calm, I remained quiet, dealt with the inward "cracks," and kept moving forward. I was still *Broken,* not healed nor delivered. I was still going to church, playing music, preaching, helping my Aunt Michelle direct the choir, and doing all I could to stay *saved* and *sane.*

It was the third Sunday in May, and the service was amazing! Probably one of the greatest services I've ever attended. After service, my wife went to a baby shower, and I felt exhausted from working all week and weekend, so I decided to take my two children and go home to lay down and rest. I remember on the way home, my two-year-old daughter and I were singing a popular song that was playing on the radio while she was secured in her child seat, and my five-month-old was asleep in his car seat. That was the last thing I remembered. When I woke up, I had an IV hooked up to my arm, multiple stickers and wires stuck to my chest for EKG purposes, and a clear tube blowing air into my nose.

As I gained consciousness, I thought, "Where the heck am I?" I tried to sit up but noticed I was strapped to the bed. My church shirt was missing buttons as though it had been ripped open. When my eyes were opened clearly, the doctor informed me that I was in the hospital. I had been in a car accident.

I first thought, "Oh, My God, my Kids!" as I tried to sit up again.

The doctor assured me, "Your Kids are fine, Mr. Glanton. I need you to calm down, relax, please!"

I began to worry, and I could literally feel my blood pressure rise. I didn't see any familiar faces; I didn't even know if I was safe. I felt myself drifting back to sleep. When I woke up again, I was still in the hospital, and the first person I saw was my mother; she was holding my daughter. As I turned my head and scanned the room, I saw a Caucasian guy, not dressed in scrubs but wearing brown jeans and a white t-shirt. I tried to speak my words, inquiring about the whereabouts of my son; my mom answered, "He's ok. They're just doing additional tests to make sure he's fine."

In the cutest little voice, my daughter asked, "Daddy, are you ok?"

I shook my head "yes," and she said, " You broke my knee, Daddy." I looked at her leg, and there was a small scratch on her knee from the accident. I started to weep because I felt like her pain was all my fault.

Then I looked at the Caucasian guy, and he began explaining to me what had happened. He told me he was driving behind me, going the same direction at about 45 miles per hour. He then noticed my car swerving back and forth. He said he tried to speed up to pass me when he saw my car drift over into oncoming traffic. He told me that he was beeping his horn like a madman, trying to get other cars attention so that they wouldn't crash into me.

As I drifted into the oncoming traffic, he said my car sped up and drifted all the way over onto the sidewalk, making a B-line towards a brick building for a head-on collision; he felt helpless because he couldn't do anything to stop it. He continued to tell me that he watched my car crash into the building, going about 52 miles per hour; its impact pushed my car back into a utility pole, which caused the pole to fall directly on the top of the vehicle. Multiple cars stopped to render help, and someone had already called 911 for an ambulance. He said although about six or seven people were sprinting to my car to help me out, he was ahead of the pack trying to rescue me, but before he could get to me, I had jumped out with both of my kids in my arms screaming, "Somebody take my babies!"

When he grabbed my daughter and another young lady grabbed my son (who was still asleep and strapped in his car seat) from my arms, I fell straight back onto the grass, and he thought I had died right there before the ambulance could arrive. However, when the EMTs arrived, the first thing they did was rip my shirt and check my blood pressure, and it was 227/144. That's when he heard one of the EMTs say, "Stroke Alert! He's had a stroke! Let the hospital know!"

He said by this time, the ambulance was on the scene, and my mother had also made it to the scene. The doctors had brought my son to me as the man continued to talk, and my mother began to thank him for being the first on-site to help me. At this point, all I could do was cry real tears as I held my son because I knew at that moment that things could've been a lot worse. The doctors determined that I had a stroke while driving due to my high blood pressure problems.

God brought my children and me through that, and I was able to go home that same day. Yes, it's an amazing story to tell indeed, but that's not where the story ends. I still had to get the belongings I left in my car from a junk garage that the car was towed to. So, I asked my mom if she could go and retrieve my things. She agreed to do so.

Maybe two or three days after the accident, I'm back at work, working hard. My mother called me to inform me that she had my things. As I thanked her for getting my stuff, I noticed her voice sounded like she had been crying. I ask, "What's wrong, Momma?"

She replied that nothing was wrong, but she needed me to get my things after work. Now, remember, I didn't have a car, so I took the bus over to my parent's house after work. When I arrived at my parent's, I greeted my mom and dad and went to the basement to get my stuff. My mother followed me down the stairs; she pulled out her phone and showed me three pictures on her phone. The first picture was a picture of my car in between the brick building and the utility pole, with the pole resting on top of my car. The second picture, I believe, was a picture she took of my car while at the garage that showed the overall external damage to the front that resulted from the initial contact with the brick building.

She told me when she informed the guy at the garage that she was there to retrieve my things, the man offered his condolences to her because he thought I had died in the crash.

When my mom informed him that I was alive and God was good, he took her to the driver's side of my car and told her to "look in." which brings me to the third picture. It was a picture of the inside of my car where you can see the car's engine just nearly in the front seat of my car. Which made me think, "How in the world did I get out of this car after impact?" A better question was, "How did I get my kids out of the car?" as close as that engine was to the driver's seat, based on that picture my mother showed me, my legs would've burned all the way to the bone from a hot engine resting on my legs. *Yet I walked out of the accident with my kids safely. No bumps, bruises, no scars, or burns.* THANK YOU, JESUS!

I remember testifying at church, showing those pictures on the big screen; so the church could see for themselves how God literally spared our lives. And you already know, we danced a while in that Sunday morning service. **MISSION FAILED.**

Chapter Six

I could literally write all day, for an eternity talking about the goodness of Jesus, and I can testify till kingdom come here on earth about how real God is in my life. We sometimes fail to realize that there must be **tests** to bring about **test**imonies. There must be struggles to witness the victories. We must experience pain in order to display HIS true *power*. Sure, during the tested times we face, during the struggles we experience, and through the pain we endure, the last thing we want to hear is "For God So Loved the World"*(John 3:16)*. Speaking from personal experiences, I knew the word of God. I studied the gospel of Jesus. I knew what, **2 Timothy 3:12 (KJV)** says, "***Yea and all that will live godly in Christ Jesus shall suffer persecution.***" However, when you're in the trenches, fighting off attacks, and struggling to be happy, not only with yourself but also with God, there are little things we refuse to cease within ourselves to allow God to take us through them with an already assured victory. My biggest struggle was pride, and accountability, Which brings me to the most critical part of life.

I was 35 years old. Life itself was beating me down, and at this point, it was a real struggle. I was still saved, and Holy Ghost filled, still traveling as an evangelist. I was still married with three children, but the fire was gone out. I felt like there was no fight left in me. Those cracks on the inside that I hid for years were beginning to surface, and truthfully, I wasn't the person I was when the Lord first saved me. I was a totally different man. I hope y'all don't mind if I can be transparent and tell the truth. I started to experience real-life struggles at home, at work, on the road, and EVEN at church. The warfare was REAL, ladies and gentlemen; it seemed like I was fighting demons EVERYWHERE, every step I took. I was tired, and honestly, I wanted OUT.

I remember preaching my last message in Dallas, Texas. I remember the feeling that night when I got back to my room, crying and asking God, "All this and for what? This is way too overwhelming for me, and I CAN'T DO THIS ANYMORE! So, I'm just going to step back from this (preaching) and focus on just making my music."

I mean, can you imagine that? After all, God had done for me up to this point in my life, I, Durmond Lavell Glanton, had the nerve to tell God how it's going to be for my life from this point moving forward? I must've been crazy, right? No, that wasn't the case. I had allowed Satan to take control of my mind, my spirit, and most importantly, my heart. So, by the time I returned home from this particular trip, I had zero tolerance for any foolishness, even though I was full of foolishness.

I started to make it known to everyone around me that, for the moment, I was done preaching, and my music was priority number one. Some people understood, and many thought I was crazy, but for the most part, it wasn't an intelligent decision on my behalf. What made the situation worse for me was that my whole life up to this point, I based all my decision-making on the opinions of the ones I loved and NOT what God was telling me to do. I could've easily told them throughout my life, even when my spirit became vexed, that I would make decisions according to what God says. But when you become unknowingly angry and allow the devil to get in your ear, especially when you fill yourself with pride, you will start to believe that you can make it *ON YOUR OWN, withOUT God.*

The more they gave me their opinions, the more I rebelled. The more I heard *"God is NOT pleased"* from folks, the more I felt myself drifting further away from God. One day I just told myself, "I'm tired of this." I was tired of the lack of respect (so I thought). I was tired of people treating me as if I wasn't mature or strong enough to make my own decisions.

Things were rocky at home. I felt like I was doing everything by myself, including raising three kids and a grown woman. Things were also rocky at work, dealing with a boss whom I felt didn't see or know *my worth* to the company. Things were also really rocky at church. I felt like everyone depended on me – I was singing, preaching, directing the choir, playing the organ, and sometimes, multiple services in a day. Now, remember, I knew what the Bible said *according to* **Romans 12:1 (KJV), "I beseech you therefore, brethren, by the mercies of God, that ye present your bodies a living sacrifice, holy, acceptable unto God, which is your reasonable service."** But *I was literally TIRED of it, and I had enough.*

So, I thought that maybe, just maybe, I could make *myself disappear* from EVERYBODY. "I can trust *ME*," I began to tell myself. I figured if I stopped preaching, singing, playing (Organ), and doing the "church" thing, maybe then my struggles would stop. Things had just gotten too overwhelming for me, and I was tired of dealing with the internal pain from the cracks of brokenness that nobody saw. So, I did it. As everyone knew, I made myself disappear from the world of *Elder Durmond Glanton* and tried to start doing my own thing by myself. So, I stepped away from the pulpit.

I felt as though no one cared about my spiritual being or how I felt at the time. All this sanctification in the church, and no one could discern that I had a problem. They didn't care if my home was in disarray. Their only concern was for me to shut up and preach. I started turning down appointments from other pastors and churches. I walked away from the family I established through prayer and a righteous living. I felt like in my home; no one cared about what was happening on the inside; as long as I could smile and say, "God is good," nothing else mattered. However, I refused to come to church or be out in public and pretend that everything was fantastic at the house. I just walked away from God. It ended up being the BIGGEST mistake I've ever made in my entire life.

I arranged to stay with a friend until I was able to get myself together, but that didn't work out as planned. It was not even three days after making this decision I lost the job that I had worked for 13 years. That one hit me hard because I never did anything to lose the job. I was the most experienced worker there. I always punched in on time; worked double shifts during the week and weekends. I was an integral and reliable employee. I felt that the job would always be there for me. Inconveniently, the job started downsizing, and I was the first to get a pink slip. So why didn't I just go back home? Because Satan had me believing that I was at the point of no return. "Don't be a punk, Durmond! Be a man. You've made your decision; now stick with it," he told me.

Before I even knew it, days turned into weeks and months, and I found myself walking the streets of my hometown, homeless. I had no resources, was barely eating, and when I didn't have a friend to sleepover at their house, I was sleeping on a park bench. My life was headed in a downward spiral.

One night around 10 pm, I walked past a known bad neighborhood. I walked past this guy, and we began to chat. I could tell by his posture that he was a drug dealer. I won't get into many details about it, but as we began to speak, I told him about my situation, and he reached in his pocket and gave me a few dollars.

I walked right over to a nearby fast-food restaurant and got some food.

As I walked the streets more, day after day, the guy and I became cool on a first-name basis. One day as I walked past him, he asked me if I needed some "bread," which I knew at the time meant "money."

I told him "yes," and he gave me a bag and told me to sell it for him.

The bag was filled with cocaine. I agreed to do so, and he pointed me in the direction that I should sell it. I did that and brought him back the earnings for it, and he gave me a portion of the money, just like that. Simple and easy. As time went by, he supplied me with a gun and more cocaine, and I found myself doing things I never wanted to do; posting up at a local gas station every day, selling cocaine, drinking, and partying with the brother I met, and some of his associates.

Before I knew it, I was selling cocaine, addicted to cocaine, and drinking alcohol excessively every day to numb the spiritual pain and "prove" that I was not that "church boy" that everybody thought they knew. Stupid, right? However, as rebellious as I was at the time, I *knew* the saints that *knew* me were praying for my deliverance. I was going through it y'all. It had got so bad that I would look in the mirror and not recognize who I was.

NOW, by this time (I didn't realize it yet), the internal cracks had fallen through, and I was officially **broken.** I didn't like the person I had become; snorting coke all day, drinking heavy liquor, and smoking marijuana every day. Trying to hide who I was, but guess what? If I drop a $20 bill on the ground and cover it with dirt, leaves, grass, or whatever, underneath all that stuff, it's STILL a $20 bill, and you know what? That 20 *still* has its value. *Man, that just preached right there!*

My mom always told me, "Durmond, you can try to be in the streets all you want to, but you'll never be *street* material."

So, I sat on a cold floor in a homeless shelter, staring off into space; I started to reflect on my life. Can I be honest with y'all? I hated the person I had become.

Suddenly, one Thursday night, I completely snapped; I got tired of living! I had no resources; the "friends" I thought I had were not really my friends because they really didn't even truly know me, and I'm not going back to the pulpit, Period. I began to feel an evil spirit take control of my mind as I thought to myself, "That's it! I'm going to church this Sunday, get prayer, leave the church, come back to this shelter, and find a way to end my life." That was my plan from that moment, heading into the weekend and attending church "*one last time.*"

And let me tell you, that weekend before the final Sunday, I partied like it was my last weekend on earth. In my mind, quite frankly, it was. Since this is it, I figured I might as well go all out. The "friends" I was hanging with had NO idea where my mind was. It was GONE y'all.

So, here we are; it's Sunday morning, the *final Sunday* morning. I woke up early at like 6 am and went to the restroom to start shaving myself clean. As I shaved, I remember thinking to myself, "When my body is being viewed in my coffin, my head would be nicely shaved." The Devil really had my mind.

I got dressed, got picked up by my boy, who was the church drummer and headed out to the church, where it all began for me as a four-year-old drummer—one last time. My homeboy and I didn't have much conversation on the way there. We were just listening to the local radio playing gospel on Sunday mornings.

When I got to the church, the first person I saw was my Aunt Michelle, the choir director. She hugged me and told me how much she had missed me. She also said, "See me before you leave, nephew. I got something to give you."

By this time, everyone was coming to greet me and displaying excitement to see me. I thought they were all phony and really didn't care how I was doing. They had NO CLUE, the evil thoughts I had in my head as I walked into the sanctuary and took my seat towards the back. I didn't want to deal with anybody. I just wanted to hug my mom one last time before ending my life.

There isn't much I can remember about the service that day, but I do remember seeing the saints dance and having some good church. I remember my Godfather preaching a powerful dynamic message. However, nothing moved me. I still sat in the pew as a broken man. When it was time for the altar call, my mother signaled for me to come to get prayer. I thought, "Ok, that's cool, one last prayer."

As I stood at the altar with about 15 other people, my Godfather began to pray. I never closed my eyes to pray; I just stood at the altar looking and waiting for him to finish so I could get back to my seat. Then, he came and laid his hand on my forehead and began rebuking all kinds of demons and spirits, but I chose to still rebel, although once he laid his hand on my head, I closed my eyes and figured I'd better pray a little. The next thing I know, I felt hands on my shoulders, back, legs, feet, chest, and stomach. When I opened my eyes, there were at least 50-65 saints crowded around just me at the altar. The rest of the church surrounded them, had their hands on me, and were crying out on my behalf. At THAT moment, I started to cry. I remember crying so hard, not because I felt God touch me, but because I knew I would be just a memory by the following Sunday. That's pretty much all I remember from the actual service that day. After service, I hugged almost everyone I could get my hands on to say my goodbyes, especially my mother.

I got in my boy's car to leave, eyes bloodshot from the tears. As we were leaving the church parking lot to go back to the shelter and then death, my Aunt Michelle waved us down to stop us before pulling off. She reached in her pocket and pulled out a blank CD. No words on it, no barcodes, just a blank CD. She handed it to me and said, "Here, Durmond. Take this, and if you don't do ANYTHING ELSE today, please listen to this song on here. Promise me."

I said, "Ok, Auntie, I promise I'll listen to it." and put the CD in my pocket, not even thinking about it.

So, I got back to the Ave and called one of my spiritual mothers for a word of encouragement. After hanging up with her, I went across the street to the liquor store, got a few drinks to numb myself, chugged them all, and headed for the shelter to take a bottle of pills and die in my sleep (man, I'm in tears writing this).

As I got to the shelter, I chilled in the lobby area, where there were about eight (8) others there with the boom box playing. I don't know why; I can't even explain it to this day, but I asked the brothers there if I could listen to a CD real quickly before going to bed. I wanted to make good on my promise to my aunt. After getting clearance to use the radio, I plugged in the headphones, popped in the CD, and pushed play. Let me tell y'all something; I couldn't stop crying listening to this song. I felt like God Himself was talking DIRECTLY to me.

Yes, the song on that CD SAVED MY LIFE! Regarding the artist, I won't tell y'all what song it was, but I decided that I didn't care how long it took me; I would get up, get myself together, and take back my life.

I told God out loud, "Lord, if you allow me to survive through the night, I'll go get help first thing in the morning."

I spent most of the night fighting for my life, a straight tug of war between my life and my death, crying so hard and staring at the bottle of pills. The devil told me, "Go ahead and stick by your words like a man. DO IT! Take 'em ALL!"

God told me, *"Throw those things (the pills) away. SURVIVE AND LIVE!"*

It was the longest six hours of my life—a war between my flesh and my spirit. The broken man was pulling me toward death, and the man of God was pulling me toward life. The prayer of the earlier church service from the saints played a HUGE role in me choosing to live while on the floor of that shelter that night. **James 5:16 (KJV)** states that ***"The prayers of the righteous availeth much."*** Thank you, Jesus! I began to ask the Lord to help me.

The spirit of death was definitely lurking around me. I felt it, and I knew I was very close to it. Then God began to give me strength, and I began to decree to myself that *"I'm not going to die! I deserve to live!"* all night long, and because it ***felt different,*** I felt that God delivered my mind, my heart, and most importantly, my brokenness, right there in that shelter room. I was happy to make it to the next morning. I MADE IT; I SURVIVED!

As promised, I got up, got dressed, and headed out to go to the social services department to try and get some help. But be clear, the devil will try to retaliate when God delivers. As I was on my way riding the city bus, I felt my entire left side go numb; I remember stomping my left foot so hard to get feeling back in it; next thing I know, I opened my eyes and found myself back on top of a hospital bed. Yep, you guessed it, I had a stroke and was hospitalized for six (6) days not being able to use my left side, and let me tell you something, when you are flat on your back like that, there's not too much to do but pray and write. And that's exactly what I did, right on that hospital bed.

I promised God that if He gave me another chance, "THIS TIME, I'll do it the right way."

Chapter Seven

Isn't it funny, though? Sometimes when we find ourselves in desperate need and dire straits, we make promises to God and then go back on them. I can't speak for anyone else concerning this manner, only myself. After taking combinations of medicine and intense physical therapy for a few days, my health somewhat got back on track, but my spirit was still messed up. So, here's where my life got tricky. Are you listening to me?

After five days of being in the Stroke Unit in the hospital, my body gained strength, and I was cleared to leave the hospital and go home. Let me say this; it's a huge mistake to display deliverance, especially to others, and still NOT be fully recovered from your brokenness. In my defense, coming from the hospital, I believed that I was completely delivered. Not only that, I was excited to let people know that God set me free from the streets, which was true, but was I delivered from my self-consciousness? Was my life re-dedicated back to God? Have I completely let go of my anger? Did I learn how to forgive genuinely?

I remember growing up in the church; this one specific mother would always say, "When we forgive, we must throw it in the sea of forgetfulness, and put a sign out there that says, "NO FISHING." That's pretty deep, isn't it? I never understood it until I got older. So again, I was cleared to go home from the hospital.

Things still weren't great at home in my marriage, so I stayed at my parents' house until I could figure out my next move in life. I spent many days and nights crying, frustrated, pointing fingers, and dishing out blame. To me, I felt like everyone was against how I felt. I mean, come on, people, I just got out of the hospital from having a stroke; before that homeless on the street, and nobody was coming to my defense in this marriage?

One person (who will remain nameless) who was a church member had the nerve to tell me that what I'd been through up to that point was only because I was *reaping what I sowed.* Now again, I know I wasn't perfect as a husband, but I'm almost sure, not 100% confident, but almost sure that I wasn't alone as far as the things that went sour in my home. So many times, I wanted to explode with fury on those who thought I was a dirty dog but thought she was innocent. However (here's the tricky part), I had already put it out to everyone that I was *delivered* and *set free,* right? So, guess what I had to do? Instead of "holding everything in" and remaining *cool,* I started compartmentalizing my emotions this time.

I wore a constant smile to prove to everyone that I had changed for real. The crucial mistakes I made were simple yet critical. Looking back on it now, I wonder, why didn't I pray when I got these feelings? Men ought ***"Always to Pray"*** and not faint, right? So why didn't I talk to God about it? Even when I returned to church, why did it take me so long to show gratitude to God in His house for saving my life? But yet and still, I was proclaiming to everyone that I was delivered.

After about a month and a half home from the hospital, I sat in Sunday morning service at the church. I was sitting near the back while service was going on. I remember the moment I was sitting there furious on the inside, not being fully delivered like I'd told everyone. I was frustrated thinking about how I was being ridiculed as a husband, but who I was married to was being treated like a victim in this entire situation. It just didn't seem right to me, and I began to spew the vibe in the atmosphere that the church folks were too phony for me.

As I sat there with my arms folded, the service was at an all-time high. The people were dancing, the music was cranking, people were taking laps around the church, and here I am during it all, sitting with my arms folded. I was halfway frustrated and halfway embarrassed. Why? Remember, I was just preaching to these people not too long ago, now I'm back here, and they know where I've been; the lies were already spread about me and what I've done. I was too irritated and too embarrassed to even clap my hands.

Then suddenly, out of nowhere, I felt a ball of fire hit my lower back like a bullet, and an overwhelming spirit came over me that caused me to cry. Then I heard a voice as clear as day say, "Really, Durmond? You're really sitting here in MY house, you KNOW I'm here, and you're not gonna give me praise? You're worried about what these church folk are thinking concerning you when I was the one who brought you out and saved your life?"

That's all I needed to hear. I jumped up out of my seat while the praise was in the air, and I *finally* thanked God for saving my life.

Before I knew it, I was at the altar on my knees, asking Him to forgive me and save me all over again. I wept and cried, hollered and wailed, and it happened. God gave me a second chance to live for Him. And even until this day, no matter what I go through or experience, if I can't find anything else, I know how to find a praise.

For the moment, I was refreshed, replenished, and genuinely happy for the first time in a long time. Nevertheless, there still was a problem. I was saved, yes, but I still had a rocky marriage. I still dealt with things that caused me to get angry and frustrated. It wasn't until I sat down and spoke with my father about it, who wasn't saved, but I trusted his wisdom and advice. I remember telling him how I was starting to dislike church and the people there.

As we sat out front of the house in his pickup truck, I began to express to him how everyone seemed to be blaming me for what was wrong in my marriage and treating "her" like she was some broken woman that did nothing wrong and was loyal and dedicated to being a wife to me. This man looked me in the face and said, "Durmond, aren't you a preacher? You know the word, right? You mean to tell me you know God, and you didn't **pray** and talk to Him about it?"

I mean, wow! Like really, WOW! I had no answer for him, but he was absolutely right! My dad reminded me that I had to talk to Him to know God for myself. It's what separates **Religion** from **Relationship.** I can go to church every day of the week, shout, dance, preach or pray. However, if I don't communicate with God through prayer and supplication, I'm just caught up in the emotions of **religion**.

Eventually, I ended up trying to reconcile things with my wife, but by then, there was too much collateral damage. She had been in another intimate relationship, and I felt that if she had taken the time and effort to look for me while I was homeless, she wouldn't have had the time to be in another relationship. But God knows, and we still tried to make the marriage work. I want to make this very, very clear. When you choose to work on a relationship with your spouse, you must learn to forgive, first and foremost, and honestly, I had a problem doing that.

I got the bright idea that maybe God could change me spiritually if I could physically get out of my comfort zone. I was at the point of no return; I didn't want to be a part of the church I'd been with my whole life. I was tired of the members, and quite frankly, I was still bitter about how I felt done wrong by them. By feeling that way, I spent a lot of Sundays in church angry with the saints rather than using that energy towards my praise and worship. I was tired of everyone telling me what was right or wrong according to God's will for my life, and I figured I had to move far away from the equation for that to stop. So, that's what I did, I packed a few weeks' worth of clothes, and I moved from Rochester, New York, to Atlanta, Georgia. Far, far away, without telling a single soul.

Chapter Eight

For years, I allowed others to make decisions for my life; I was tired of it and wanted a fresh start. My sister was pastoring in Atlanta and was looking for an organist. I felt it was an opportunity to grow musically and spiritually. Again, for a short-lived moment, I was happy and excited to start fresh. For a while, I was growing; I was making money, playing music, and pursuing a career as a Gospel artist. It started promising; I connected with a local radio promoter who adored my song and thought I could rise to the top. And you know what? I bought into it.

After hearing that ignited a fire in me to make it because, by this time, everyone knew in NY that I snuck out of town and moved elsewhere. Some were excited, but most were confused and not too happy with me because not many people knew. Secondly, my wife and kids were still in New York, which was a no, no to them. So, I had a choice to make. Do I bring them down to Georgia with me, or do I move on with my life? Alone. After all, I was still broken. I couldn't seem to shake the anger from the betrayal I felt. I figured that if she's not around, there's nothing to forgive, right? But for once in my life, I wanted to do something the right way. My children were missing me, and I was missing them. When I would call, my daughter would cry and beg me to please come back home.

Although there was a lot of collateral damage, as a father, I didn't want to put my kids through the pain of growing up without a dad as I did somewhat. Speaking for myself, I had no father until the age of eight. It was just my mother and my brothers. My biological father lived in Florida, and I never saw him. That was a different kind of pain for my brother Johnnie and me. I felt unwanted as a son to him, worthless, and not good enough to be in his life. I didn't know it then, but I kept quiet and kept it all in. What once was heartbreak turned into pure anger the older I got, still not hearing from him. I promised myself that if I ever had children, I would never bring pain to them as a father as this man had brought to me. So, long story short, I prepared to take a quick trip back home to get my family and bring them to Georgia for all of us to start fresh and leave whatever happened in New York *in New York*.

Sometimes a good idea should just remain a good idea. Let me explain. It's very difficult to move when God gives you a "cathedral" vision and the ones on your team who are supposed to have your back have a "storefront" mentality. I was excited about a new start in a new city. I was ready to put the pedal to the metal and work so hard to put my family in a position never to struggle again. The problem with this scenario was simple, and hear me clearly, brothers and sisters, if you ever decide to move forward from past pain, you MUST leave that pain where you left it, *in the past*. It's important to know this because if everyone on your team isn't on the same page as you, it will be very difficult to obtain any victories.

What am I saying? Moving to Georgia, I had a plan, a vision; I knew what I was going to do, how I was going to do it, and the outcome of me doing what I had to do. However, my wife, at the time, wasn't too keen on moving out of state. She was content with the family support in New York; she was set in the church in New York and was rightfully fearful of uprooting everything she was used to and moving far away from it. Obviously, like any spouse who wasn't on the same page as their mate, she bucked and rebelled against the grain. She didn't want to move.

At that moment, I didn't care about compromise or listening to any opinions. I wanted *out* of Rochester, this was my opportunity, so I was gone! So let me be responsible and accountable by saying this, I was wrong in how I moved. Marriage is about compromise and valued opinions. It's about finding common ground to work together towards a common goal. I didn't care because in my mind, "This is what God told me, and I'm going to FINALLY move on God's word and NOT on the opinions of people."

I'd totally forgotten what I had learned. **Colossians 3:13 (KJV)** *says,* ***"Bear with one another and, if one has a complaint against another, forgive each other; as the Lord has forgiven you, so you also must forgive,"*** and **Ephesians 5:25 (KJV)** *says,* ***"Husbands, love your wives, just as Christ loved the church and gave himself up for her."*** But at this point in my life, I felt like I'd done everything I could as a husband and father and that it was time for me to be obedient to Him that called me.

What upset me about this whole situation was that, as long as I was preaching what people wanted to hear (which was the gospel), they were satisfied and knew I was hearing from God. But the moment I would put in the atmosphere that God was pulling me towards a direction they weren't familiar with, then it wasn't God talking but the enemy. So, my thing was, wait, hold on, you mean to tell me I can hear the same voice on two separate occasions and two separate instructions, but one is God, and the other is the Devil? The same voice I listen to encourage and make y'all shout and dance all over the sanctuary isn't the same voice that told me to get out of my comfort zone and move?

So, it slowly started to occur to me that the support I thought I was getting was *conditional;* and at the end of the day, when I stand in judgment before God Himself, I will have to give an account for my actions. I totally disregarded every opinion that rose against what I wanted to do, including my wife's views.

Chapter Nine

I was happy and excited to start from scratch for the first couple of months in Georgia *with* my wife and kids. I had left everything that caused me pain back in NY and started seeing things from a more positive perspective. I was maximizing the time spent with my children and my wife. I figured this was the start of rekindling and reconciling any damage that was broken beyond repair. I knew one day; we would have a story to tell to help other broken marriages; that was the plan, right? Then things started to change.

We stopped talking, there was really no connection, and I felt that her heart turned on me. Again, I moved forward, agreeing not to involve the past hurt from whence I came, but as previously stated, if you and your spouse aren't on the same wave, the connection will be lost, and that's what happened. I received an enormous phone bill tripled in price, so I went online to see why and was gut-punched by reality. My wife had an entirely different relationship with another man, including private meetings and secret rendezvous. I remember the fire in my eyes when I figured it all out. Was I hurt? Absolutely, but the anger I felt overtook me, and I completely snapped. It was the last straw. I confronted her, and I lost my cool when everything was finally exposed.

I remember picking up a chair and throwing it across the room, shattering it into pieces. It was my opportunity to **forgive**, right? Easier said than done. I miserably failed the test as I screamed and yelled; I took her belongings, threw them out of the front door, and told her to get out. I had enough at this point. Now let me say this because I was totally wrong for reacting this way. I should've never put her out in the cold and told her to "call him" it was wrong, and my children didn't need to see that, but I was fed up, ladies and gentlemen. I was completely broken; all the "healings" and "deliverances" had been annihilated. I was crushed. My plan had failed.

As I look back at it now, I couldn't really blame her for her mind still being in New York.

My argument was this, "If your mind was in New York, then you should've stayed in New York."

I had transformed from a man who was once so caring, forgiving and compromising into a cold-hearted, pain-driven, careless man who wanted out of the relationship. I left her outside all night as she tried to come back in.

Even when she screamed, "I'm sorry, please forgive me!" While banging on the door to come back inside, I sat in my living room with purely evil intentions not to let her back in. I had sacrificed so much and endured too many things to feel so betrayed and hurt by the one who was supposed to have my back and support me, but admittedly, I was dead wrong for doing this. That wasn't godly, forgiveness had left my heart at this point, and truthfully, I didn't care if she froze to death outside all night long. Eventually, I did the noble thing and let her back into the house, I was still upset, but I felt that allowing her back in was a sign of forgiveness, right? Absolutely not! Forgiveness is throwing it into the sea of "forgetfulness" with the sign that says, "No Fishing," Remember? Well, that's not what I did.

The more I saw her, the angrier I became, and the angrier I became, the more I questioned her whereabouts. That's not how marriage works. I knew that, but remember, I stopped caring. The only thing left to do was to separate. I told her she needed to go back to New York and regroup. This is what really hurt my heart. I knew the only way to get this woman out of my life I would have to say goodbye to my children. But by any means necessary, I had to get her out of my life because I was not moving back to New York.

So, she packed the things that she was able to retrieve from the front yard, put the kids' stuff in a suitcase, and headed for the bus station to move back to New York. Here's the heartbreaker for me, my kids were completely crushed to leave me. My daughter Itayvia was 12 at the time, and she cried her eyes out, "Daddy, I wanna stay with you!" was all she kept saying as the tears streamed down her face.

Even my son, Daeshon, who never really showed emotion, cried. "I don't want to go back to New York," he pleaded. The moment that my heart turned back to anger was when I looked up while hugging my children, only to see my wife smiling and smirking as if it was a big joke. *Now* I full-blown hated this woman. To see the pain in your kids' faces, knowing how they feel about me, and knowing I've been with them their entire lives, and you're smiling? Yep, I hate you.

Watching them board the bus was equivalent to watching Iyana's casket lowered into the ground. I felt like I was losing my children again. I was done; my heart was full of hatred. I left the bus station in tears, not knowing if I'll ever see my children again. I started to feel like I'd lost the battle. My life was going down the same road; the situation triggered me to hit the streets again.

I started walking the streets of Stone Mountain; I didn't want to sleep in the house anymore. There was a gas station outside of the complex, and I took every dime I had and started buying alcohol to numb my pain. My sister, Yolonda, would come looking for me, and I was gone. The complex landlords would tell her that they barely saw me and I didn't look stable. I was back at square one. The last time I felt this way, I wanted to end my life. My family was gone, and my children (who were my life) were gone. What was the point of living? I had given up the fight.

I remember calling my mother, and at the time, she was in the process of being installed as a church mother. I felt the same way I felt while homeless, "I have to go see my parents and my kids one last time." So, with some extra money, I booked a flight to go home and see my family, then come back to Atlanta.

A couple of nights before my trip back home, I was on the phone with my brother Johnnie, and as I began to explain to him what I've been going through and how I felt, he began to fuel my anger, but more so positively. How is that possible? That sounds like an oxymoron, right? He began to tell me to use my anger as motivation, get off my behind, and make it happen for ME. That may sound a little selfish, but that seemed to be the only way I would survive this heartbreak. He then began to tell me to meet new people and create a new circle.

"How, Johnnie? I'm not the type, never been the type to go online to look for friends."

He told me to download an app on my phone that he often uses. "What? No, man, I'm not doing that, bro!"

He made me promise to reach out on this app and talk to someone. He informed me that I had to get a lot off my chest, and so that I could get back on track, I had to "Let it off, then let it go." That advice ended up being life-changing for me.

So, with a broken heart and a no-trust zone, I downloaded the app to reach out to people I didn't even know to converse about the pains of my life. It sounds completely ridiculous, but whatever, I'll do it to make good on my word to my brother; after all, I am my brother's keeper. Let me tell y'all something, the very FIRST face I saw on this app happened to be a very attractive female with a gorgeous smile, red hair, and a trusting look.

"Eeeh, ok, I'll send her a message; you might as well reach out." I sent a simple message just saying, "Hello."

Before I could even go to the next person, she responded, "Hello, how are you?"

I spent the entire night talking with this young lady, we had so many things in common, and we could connect on many levels. We exchanged numbers, locked each other's names and numbers in our phones, and deleted the app before I went to bed. My work was done. I had found a new friend. We spent a lot of time talking, laughing, and comparing life stories the next few days. Even when I went to NY to see my mom installed as a church mother, we kept in contact. I found myself so comfortable talking with this woman I wanted to get the opportunity to actually meet her. I mean, you can say I was wrong for looking for new friends being a married man; maybe you're right, but I was done with this marriage. I wanted no parts of it anymore. I hated her and didn't want anyone trying to talk me into going back to a marriage. I was over. I was content with the conversations with my new friend.

Whenever I saw my then soon-to-be ex-wife in New York, I barely said two words to her; my hatred towards her was evident and real. I enjoyed hugging and kissing my children, rooting my mom on, kicking it with my father, and enjoying the rest of my family. I was still stand-off-ish towards anyone who seemed cool with her, including some family members. I felt that the church was believing her lies and rumors and siding with her like she was some victim. I KNEW the truth; then, I didn't want any parts of them either. Everyone was an enemy at this point. But I had a friend to talk to, so I didn't care. This is what I wanted. When you're in pain and your heart is broken, whether you love God or not, the last thing you want to hear is, "**The Lord is my Shepherd.**" I'm just trying to be as transparent as possible. I must tell the *truth* in order to free myself. It is the ***TRUTH* that makes us free,** right?

I was so angry that I thought of ways to get back at her and everyone supporting her, including my family members; I wanted revenge; I aimed to hit every moving target. **Romans 12:19** (KJV) ***"Dearly beloved, avenge not yourselves, but rather give place unto wrath: for it is written, Vengeance is mine; I will repay saith the Lord."*** These are things I knew;

scriptures that I'd preached for years; and quotes that I strived to live by.

When it was time to apply what I knew, why did I move the opposite way? Because when you have been broken, and when you have openly been broken, sometimes you find yourself on the defense, and to protect who you believe you are, especially from a place of hurt, you don't care who you hurt. Plain and simple. Misery loves company, and now this my was my state of mind. "I'm coming back to hurt everyone that hurt me in life."

I had temporarily lost my entire cool. Everyone would feel it, and I didn't care, just like I thought they didn't care about my pain. To be honest, I had serious anger issues with the church that I'd known my whole life. It was like they knew what I was going through and still sided with who I considered was my enemy. That's how I felt, so that's how I decided to treat the situation as such.

As soon as the installation service was over, I wanted to get back to Atlanta to start my new life, but no one knew. I stopped answering phone calls and began blocking people on social media; some were even family members. I was just done with everybody.

This brings me to my next point. It was so unfair for me to channel the anger I carried from the past into what I thought was a real fresh start. Remember, I met someone; I didn't even want to bring any family members into my life anymore or reconnect with anyone associated with my old life in New York. So, once again, I made myself disappear. Sure, I talked with my mom, dad, and brothers occasionally. But this was MY LIFE, and for once, I wanted to do what I wanted, talk to whoever I pleased and enjoy the rest of my life *without family*.

Chapter Ten

I began to talk and pour out my true feelings onto my new friendship with the young lady I met online. The more we conversed, the more I felt I could trust her. We had met for dinner a few times by now, and even when I was reluctant to open up and expose my broken heart, she would look me in the eye and always say, "Durmond, I'm not afraid of you. I'm not here to hurt you, I'm a loyalist, and if I tell you I got you, you can take it to the bank because I really got you."

Those were words I always wanted to hear. So, the **interest** I had in her slowly became **like**, and the more time I spent with her daily, the **like** grew into **love.** Within three months, I got a divorce and finally felt free. I started to put all my time and energy towards this phenomenal young lady who I now publicly made my lady, and by the tenth month, I decided to make her my wife.

Now let me tell you something: I had no one to turn to during those recovering moments. I blamed the world and the church for everything I'd gone through up to that point. I still hated my ex-wife; truthfully, I wanted her dead; and I still stayed away from family and made it a point to be content with any decision I made concerning my life. This woman had my back through it all; she loved me unconditionally, she made me a part of her world, and even though I was missing my children tremendously (mainly because of my own hatred), she allowed me to love her eight-year-old daughter as if she was my own. I had become "family " with them. My heart mattered to them; they valued my opinions.

Here's the "hook, line, and sinker," once my lady found out what all I'd done for a living before meeting her; being a musician and a preacher, she told me flat out, "Well, we're going to get you back to doing that, because if this is what God wants you to do, then you're going to do it because I don't want any bad *'juju'* coming back on us as a unit because of your disobedience and decision not to follow what God wants."

Although it was an amazing way of thinking on her behalf, I wasn't buying it y'all. I told her on many occasions just to shut her up, "Yea, ok, babe, I'll get back to it one day." Intending never to touch a mic again, whether it was music or preaching. But one thing this beautiful young lady taught me throughout our friendship and now the relationship is **Consistence brings Existence.**

She was determined to get me back on track by showing support and making connections with new people in different arenas. It was like she moved with the fear of God. Support, genuine support is all I ever needed to get me back on track. I feel very comfortable saying this, the way she loved me changed me as a man. Not a Man of God, but just a man. I changed; her love for me taught me to forgive. Even when I would call and check on my children and had to talk to the woman I despised the most, I found myself handling the situations between the two of us with grace, growth, and maturity.

The love of my "soon to be wife" brought to my attention that being upset with my ex and hating her doesn't help ME grow as a man. I had someone special in my life now. I was the happiest I'd ever been in my life. The thought of my hatred towards my ex made me hate her as my ex even more. But if I moved on, why did I hate her so much? I should thank her for breaking my heart and moving on, right?

I remember calling my dad for advice. My dad was the rawest, realest dude you'll ever meet. I remember telling him how I loved this woman, hated my ex but needed to stay cool because of my kids. And if you knew Mr. Thurman Harrell Sr. (My dad), you knew he would give it to me straight with NO chaser. He kept it 100 (*real*) with me and said, "Man, if this woman is who you wanna be with, whether the family agrees, it's ultimately YOUR choice. Even if the family is still cool with your ex, it's no longer your concern. Your concern is to the woman loving you the way you deserve to be loved. Put all religion and church aside, nigga, this is YOUR life, YOUR heart. If this is who does it for you, BE WITH HER! We're going to be here for you regardless. But for you to stay mad is saying you still have something there for your ex, and your current lady doesn't deserve that. So, if you're gonna be with Michele, let that past stuff go and enjoy your life with the woman you love."

Man, that was so refreshing to get that advice. Not even a month later, I proposed to my lady, and we were married a week later. It ended up being the best decision I ever made.

I married my best friend, and we're still strongly in love. I am her strength, and she is my weakness. We stand back-to-back and fight any force of evil that rises against this family God has put together. I'm a better man because of her, and this is in NO WAY disrespectful to my ex-wife because, at the end of the day, I want to see her win also, but I have accomplished MORE in life in six years being in Atlanta with Michele than in 20 years in my previous marriage. Those are facts; I'm more mature and a lot wiser, and I see things differently now.

I've learned how to forgive, even my ex. We now have civil conversations about our children. We visit with the kids more often, and now we are somewhat friends; we can laugh and joke about certain things. She has moved on, and so have I. Itayvia (my daughter) now lives in Georgia with me, and she is happy with life, which is all I care about. She and Alana, the baby girl, are two peas in a pod and very close. Alana always wanted a big sister, and Tay has always wanted a little sister. Look how God worked that out.

But there was still a problem. I was still so far from being the Man of God I once was. I was back on the music scene. Michele is now my manager, and she's keeping me busy with single releases, radio interviews, and performances at local and surrounding concerts. My name was finally starting to get a buzz in the music industry. She even got my single to #3 on the Billboard Internet Charts. She was working hard, supporting what I was doing in music ministry. However, again, there was a problem. She felt that the accomplishments weren't enough because I needed to make my way back to the pulpit preaching the gospel. I would make her so mad because when she would present a platform for me to preach on, I would tell her I wasn't ready, so my answer was always, "No."

She didn't understand that I didn't want to go through the pressure again. I didn't want to preach to phony church folks again. My heart wasn't in it anymore. I felt like my wave of music was making enough noise that I didn't really have to preach. Boy, was I wrong.

Michele would often contact my sister, Apostle Yolanda Kuykendall (who was my pastor), who I played the organ for, and tell my sister, "Durmond needs to preach!"

Like any sister/pastor, she would agree and occasionally tell me, "Bro, you need to start preaching again." I would say, "I know, sis!" but never intended on doing so.

The risk versus reward was too much for me. I didn't want to get back into it and find myself back in the same old situations being a

Man of God. I'm cool being a recording artist. I'M GOOD YA'LL! Just let me be great. Let me make music and work my way back into the "preaching" thing on my own time. If you know, like I know, though God has a way of letting "**Time**" along with occurring situations put you in predicaments to be a man/woman of your word. Trust me when I say that God has His way of getting your attention.

I then thought about Jonah. The Man of God had simple and specific instructions; **Jonah 1:1 (KJV)** *"Arise, go to Nineveh, that great city, and cry against it; for their wickedness is come up before me."* Simple, right? However, Jonah went in the opposite direction to flee God's presence. I bought a ticket at sea, got on a boat, and headed to a city called Tarshish in the *opposite* direction. This is the disadvantage of being disobedient to God. A great storm arose on the water. The storm was so catastrophic that it would swallow the ship, and everyone on board, including Jonah (who happened to be somewhere on the boat sleeping).

It made me think about what my wife Michele told me, that my disobedience to God could cause bad things, or "juju," as she called it, to happen to our family. So, was it worth it? Was it worth allowing my family to suffer from my own spiritual selfishness? But how? How does that make me "spiritually" selfish? I'm in church every Sunday playing my heart out, giving God all I have in the music. I'm spreading the gospel as an artist on stage, radio stations, live interviews, award shows, and television showcases. Not only that, but my attitude has changed. I mean, in all seriousness, without the church, the music, and all those things, I'VE BECOME A BETTER MAN all around. I've become a better husband, a better father, and a better person in the community; I changed who I was within a year. That didn't count? No, it doesn't, and let me explain why and how God broke this thing down to me.

Everything that I accomplished up to this point in HIS name, mainly the music and accolades at the W.O.W. (Winning Over the World) Church of Georgia, was still null and void because of my disobedience, and it was starting to affect not just me, but the ones around me, mainly my wife and children. I remember asking God, "Lord, how can all of this be null and void? Because I don't want to preach anymore? It's been five years since I've mounted a platform, and you've blessed me and **graced** me with so much. Please tell me how *this* is not enough."

I love that we serve a **brilliant** and **all-wise** God; He answered me and said, *"This isn't* *enough because there's no **sacrifice.***" He then led me to Romans 12:1, where it says to present our **bodies** as a **living sacrifice.** God began to show me that "**Dead sacrifices** can't get up from the altar." How powerful is that!? He also reminded me of Isaac's words to his father, Abraham, as he was being led up to be offered. "Father, I see the **wood,** I see the ***fire,*** but WHERE is the **sacrifice?**" God was saying the same thing to me; "Durmond, I see your music accomplishments, I see your humility among others, I see your gifts being used for My Glory in church, *But* WHERE is the **sacrifice?**"

And here's what really convicted my spirit. God told me, "I've blessed you tremendously, with a beautiful home, a beautiful family that loves you for real; two (2) new cars in the driveway, and your bills are always paid. I've also given you **grace** throughout the years, but remember, it's my ***mercy*** *that's everlasting (Psalm 100:5), but My **grace*** is sufficient (II Corinthians 12:9), NOT unlimited." Whew, that hit home right there, and He finished it off by saying, "If you're truly honest with yourself, Durmond, the real reason you don't want to preach anymore is that you're afraid to admit that you're still ***broken.***"

So just like Jonah, who was caught up in a storm because of his disobedience, I had a choice to make. Either stay on the ship and destroy myself and the ones on board with me, not knowing of my disobedience or be accountable and throw myself overboard into the storm to deal with the consequences of my own circumstances. Either way, I had to face the music (no pun intended).

I felt if I'm accountable for my own actions, my family won't suffer from my spiritual shortcomings. I mean, it only seems fair. Why does my family have to pay for the things I choose to or not to do? "So ok, you got me, Lord. I'll preach again." This is what I told God. I gave him an "Okay," NOT a "**Yes,**"

You may ask, "Well, D, what's the difference?"

Me saying, "Okay," was pretty much telling God, I'll pick and choose when and where I'll speak, and I'll expound on His word. There's no need for me to tune up and get everybody hype. A scripture here, a scripture there, and I'm good, right? That should fall into the category of "Preaching" again. I'll say this once and once only; God doesn't want anything part-time He wants *all of you*. THAT'S WHERE YOUR "**YES**" is. So, give God a "**Yes**" and not an "**Okay.**" I had to learn this the hard way. I've always been God's child, but my pride, disobedience, and "**okay**" caused me a lot of pain that could've been prevented. **Hebrews 5:8 (KJV)**, "*Though he were a Son, yet learned he obedience by the things which he suffered.*"

So, there I was, thinking I was getting by on my *"Okay,"* trying to convince myself that it was a *"Yes"* to God. Getting calls to preach in different areas and platforms because Michele was starting to put me all the way out there, yet I was turning them down and saying "I'm not ready yet" to prolong the inevitable. God had to get my attention, and BOY OH BOY DID HE!!

THE BROKEN VASE

Chapter Eleven

The year was 2020. Life was great; God continued the flow of blessings to my family and me. My daughter Itayvia was now living in Georgia with me, Michele, and Baby girl, Alana. Life was going by just as smoothly as can be. Even during a global pandemic, God's grace and favor were front and center in my life. Still giving God my **"Okay,"** I was giving Him enough in my mind. Not preaching the way I should've been. Making appearances on social media pages giving spiritual "opinions" to the people of God, throwing in a scripture here and there. What more was there for me to do? And if I can be honest with y'all, I believe God had gotten fed up with my foolishness. So, here's how it all unfolded.

It was December of 2020; everything was shutting down because of COVID-19. People were dying, and the death toll was at an all-time high. We were eating dinner at the table when my phone rang. I answered it after seeing it was my mother calling. Before asking her how she and my Pops were doing, she said, "Durmond, Me and your dad tested positive for this Coronavirus."

Man, WHAT? I wasn't prepared for that. I told my mom I was coming to see them.

"No, baby, you can't travel anywhere. Everything is closing down," she explained. I started to panic. What can I do? My last scheduled trip to see my parents was three months earlier in September, which was canceled due to the virus.

The last time I *actually* saw my parents was when they came to Georgia in January of 2020 to surprise the family and me for a couple of days. It was the most memorable time I had with my parents, and the kids were excited to see them. At the time, I was very adamant about spending time with my dad. I was missing him, and to see him at my door was the best feeling ever. My dad was a huge Western junkie, and I hated Westerns. But because I was glad to be with him, we stayed up all night watching "The Magnificent 7," starring Denzel Washington.

I remember talking with him during the movie about life. This was weird because we never talk during movies, especially westerns; that was a cardinal rule. But there we were, talking about where life had brought us. He was telling me that my wife (Michele) was who I needed, and he was so glad I was with someone who could match my "grind." He adored my wife. He told me this verbatim, "Man, if you ever get sick, *this* woman will take care of you. You've been doing your thing, and she's been right by your side, helping you. THAT'S the type of woman you need! You stay with her; you'll be alright nigga!" He didn't say it word for word, but I realized at that moment that he was proud of me, which made me a very happy man.

The very next evening, which was his last night in Georgia before heading home to NY. Pop and I were sitting in the backyard, enjoying a beautiful night. He began to look over and scan my backyard with admiration; anyone that knew my dad knew he was a master landscaper. He began to tell me how it would be better for my backyard if I were to change certain things and put certain plants and trees in certain places. He kept scanning and saw my gas/charcoal grill. He looked and pointed and asked, "Man, you don't cook on that grill!?"

I answered him, "Oh, yea, man, I love this grill." He was a steak/seafood lover, so I told him, "Pop, next time you come, I'm gonna grill you a steak and lobster tail."

He just chuckled and said, "Yea, I don't know, man. I don't know when that's gonna be. Me and ya momma gonna chill for a while, so it might be a long time before that happens."

I began to tease him and let him know that he'll be back way before then. He then began to tell me how beautiful my house was, and he told me to do "what I had to do" to keep this house. I promised him that I wasn't going anywhere, "I'm here for life," I assured him. It was the most intimate moment I've ever had with my dad. It was just me and him, the warm evening weather of Georgia, and great vibes the entire night.

And now I'm on the phone with my mom informing me that she and my father were positive with a deadly virus. I asked Momma to let me speak to Pop. When he got on the phone, I remember asking him, "Pop, how you are feeling?"

He assured me that he was ok. I told him I was coming to see him, and he told me, "Man, imma be alright, you gotta wait til this virus calms down, so I'll see ya when I see ya, ya know what I mean?" Followed by his signature laugh;

that was on December 29th. The next day, my mother took him to the hospital, which was a Monday morning, he was cleared to go home, but he was back in the hospital that night. This virus was no joke. However, my dad was superman to me; he was my hero, the strongest man I knew. There was no doubt in my mind that he was strong enough to overcome this virus that was exterminating a lot of people.

To be honest, **this** situation made me pray to God more; all I wanted God to do was raise my dad up. My mother was a woman who lived her life as a sanctified Holy Ghost-filled woman, and I knew she was praying. All my aunties, cousins, and family members that I knew were *sho' nuff* saved were praying. We were all calling on the prayer warriors that we knew to bombard heaven on my father's behalf. So, I was worried, but I wasn't worried. There was too much prayer on him for him not to survive this attack. **James 5:16 (KJV)** *says,* **"The effectual fervent prayer of a righteous man availeth much."** I had no other choice but to trust God and believe that He would show Himself Mighty in this specific situation. *That's all I had.* I was calling my mom every day like three or four times to check on my father, and every time she would have the same answer, " Ya, daddy is sick baby, but we gonna trust God in this." That was all I had to hold on to. My dad was going to make it.

After the first week of him being in the hospital, I called my brother Johnnie who lives in Long Beach, California. I remember telling him that I would go insane if something happened to my father. After all, he is the greatest man I know. He kept telling me, "D, just be cool, man; Momma don't need this right now. We need to be what Dad taught us to be. You know he always told us to be 'cool' and look out for ya momma, right?"

I agreed, and he then said something I'll never forget. He said, "I know one thing, when this is all over, I'm booking a flight, I'm coming home, and I'm gonna hug my dad, man."

He said it with such confidence that I convinced myself, "Hey, you know what? Imma do that too, bro! I gotta get home to just sit with him and hug him." That became my goal; I had the confidence and faith. Nothing would stop me from getting home to my dad when he got out of that hospital.

So, it's now been a couple of weeks. Pop is still in the hospital, but I didn't know his condition. But I knew people were still dying from this virus. It was January 15, 2021, we were into a new year, and I vowed to God on New Year's Eve, which was my wedding anniversary day, that before the year was over, I would be back in the pulpit, preaching the gospel. I was determined to do all the right things, especially now that I needed a miracle. Being hospitalized for a week and two days now with COVID, the odds began to stack up against my father. *I NEEDED GOD TO MOVE.*

I received a call from my Aunt Linda, my dad's younger sister. She informed me that the hospital had set up a FaceTime call for the family to see and talk to my father. I believe I had a radio interview scheduled that evening, but I canceled everything to have this moment with my dad, who I hadn't spoken to in a few weeks.

As I sat with my wife, I was able to see my dad lying on that hospital bed with a mask on. As different members chimed in to talk to him and tell him how much they loved him, I couldn't do or say anything but cry as he responded to everyone in a soft, frail voice.

"I love you, Pop," I said, and he responded, "I love you too, Durmond...Heeey Michele!"

My wife answered, "Hey Pop, love you; hang in there." She began to rub my back as tears streamed down my face. This was my hero; I've never seen him in a weak, defeated moment in my entire life until then. As the family continued to talk to Pop, I grabbed my iPad and took a screenshot of him, myself with Michele, Johnnie, and my Aunt Linda all in the picture. I still have that picture as of today.

We said our goodbyes to him; my mother kept telling my dad, "Baby remember, keep telling him 'Yes' with every breath you take," as he shook his head in agreement.

While I looked at my dad saying goodbye to us as a family, I reflected on my life with him. My parents were high school sweethearts. At the age of 16, my mother became pregnant with my oldest brother, Shaft. They welcomed him into the world in 1973. They were in love, but they were teenagers, and like in most relationships, they went their separate ways, still loving each other. They went down different paths in life. My mom moved to Florida, and Pop stayed in New York. They both moved on with their lives and met and married other loves. One would be my biological dad, John Glanton; the other would be Anne Green. Out of these unions, four beautiful babies came about; my siblings: Thurman Jr. in 1975, Johnnie in 1976, my beautiful sister Teshimi in 1977, and then I was born a few months later in 1977.

So, here's another transparent moment for me. My mom and biological father had a real rocky marriage. I don't really know the full details, but I never really knew him or even spent time with him. For the first few years that I can remember, my dad was my grandfather, Clyde Neil Sr. I lived at his house, and from what I can remember, he and my grandmother raised me until I was about five or six years old. It wasn't until I was close to 10 years old that my mom reunited with her first love and high school sweetheart. They married in 1987 and remained husband and wife for 34 years. Within those 34 years, this man advised and guided me through everything I've ever experienced. I learned how to be a "man's man" because of him, and now through my reflections on life, I was looking at the man I called my hero, lying at the point of death. He was struggling to breathe, struggling for strength, struggling to live.

I remembered Johnnie calling me right after the family hung up with my dad and saying to me, "Bro, brace yourself! Dad might not make it. This virus is strong, man."

I remember getting so upset with him. "Like, why would you just try to destroy my hope like that?"

I truly felt he was going to make it. He then began to explain to me that he had talked to our father a couple of weeks prior to our family phone call to him, in which he had a one on one with my dad and told him, "Dad, I need you to fight this thing with all of your might, this virus can kill you. Just never give up your fight." My dad's response to him was simple.

He said, "Johnnie, man, of course, I'm gonna fight. I mean, I don't wanna die, but if anything happens, I need you and your brothers to be cool."

So, Johnnie was trying to keep me cool throughout this entire ordeal. I felt like I was losing my dad, my mind, and my cool all at one moment.

On February 2, 2021, at about 6:26 PM, my phone rang. It was my aunt Linda calling from my hometown. I answered it and was blindsided by the news. She informed me that my father was now on a breathing ventilator and would not get any better. My mother and my aunts and uncles decided to take him off and let him go peacefully.

I asked why and how they could just give up on my dad. That's when I was informed that my dad initially told my mother not to keep him on a ventilator. She had to respect his wishes. I hung up the phone mad, uptight, confused, and yet again **broken.** I wasn't ready to deal with this. About an hour and a half later. They called back and told me that my hero was gone. I felt my knees buckle as I screamed and cried. I didn't understand why. Why take the only man I trusted wholeheartedly away? Why take the foundation of our entire family? What made me question God more was why O God, why? My mother is an upright woman of God. She's up EVERY morning at 5 AM, praying her heart out. She's in every service every time the church doors open. She's faithful. If ANYBODY'S prayers deserved to be answered, it was hers. So many emotions flooded my mind, and believe me when I tell you, the devil was in my ear. My dad was no longer a living soul, and I was hurt.

If I could have another transparent moment, I told God, "So many people had it and deserved to die from it because of how they lived and survived it. So, why couldn't you just heal my father in good faith?"

James 2:14-17 (KJV) says, ***"Faith without works is dead,"*** right?

The devil told me straight up, *"All this **faith** and all of this **work** is STILL **dead.**"*

Wow! How do I respond to that? Especially from a place of hurt, pain, tears, and confusion? THIS is why it's so essential to be yoked up with the **right** companion.

Michele was able to help me push past my pain by giving me sound encouragement. She told me, "Babe, you wouldn't be the man you are today, the husband and father you are at this moment, if it weren't for Pop. The best way to keep him alive is to live your life the way he would've wanted you to. We're going to miss him for sure, but allow others to see him in the way you live every day. As a phenomenal human soul."

I began to think about how right she was. I couldn't allow everything I've been through up to this point in life to be for nothing. So, I grabbed ahold of God's word. **James 4:7 (KJV)** says, ***"Submit yourselves therefore to God. Resist the devil, and he will flee from you."*** The problem that I had (I'm not afraid to admit it) was I never could **submit** to the **commitment**; therefore, I couldn't **persist** the **resist.** I'll give y'all a moment to let that sink in. So, because of that reason alone, the battles became tougher than I ever imagined, especially after losing my father.

This brings up my next point. You can NEVER get out of the Spirit or will of God and expect to defeat the devil in your flesh. I don't care how you try to maneuver or how well you strategize your game plan. It will never happen next, and women of God, I don't care how strong and independent you think your will is, I don't care how mighty you believe your mind is; you MUST remember what it says in **Zechariah 4:6 (KJV),** ***"Then he answered and spake unto me, saying, This is the word of the LORD unto Zerubbabel, saying, Not by might, not by***

***power, but by my spirit, saith the LORD of
hosts.***"

We laid my dad to rest 11 days later. Even
in writing this, I still struggle with his death.
There were so many things I wanted him to be
around for. My music was getting a good buzz,
my life was trending up on the ladder of success,
and I needed him to be present to see it all
happen. I felt like I was cheated. Yet, there was
still a problem; I still was at an ***okay*** and not a
yes when it came to getting back to the pulpit
preaching. At this point, I was like, "Whatever,
man. I'll get to it when I get to it." My dad was
gone, and I didn't care at the moment.

While in New York, preparing for my
dad's service at my parents' house, I got a phone
call from my cousin, Claretha, from Richmond,
Virginia. The church she attended was having a
revival coming up soon, and she wanted to
confirm a conversation we had a few months
back that I would be the speaker on one of the
nights. I remember saying, "***Okay,*** cuz!" Then
went back into the living room to check on my
mother.

Now keep in mind that her high school
sweetheart, father of her first child, and husband
of 34 plus years just died. She could see how
hurt and ***broken*** I was all over my face.

As I sat at her feet, she nudged my shoulder and asked, "Hey, you alright, Mont?" She smiled with tears in her eyes.

"Naw Ma, I'm not!" was my reply. I told her how I was hurting and just heard from Claretha and what she wanted me to do.

My mother, at that moment, began to encourage me to give God a *"yes."* There's something about a mother's love and wisdom, especially when walking with God. She began to explain to me how hurt she was about the events that had transpired over the past few months. However, she was able to grab ahold of the horns of the altar and find peace. She told me she was at peace, and she understood that God is all-wise and makes no mistakes.

I couldn't figure out how she could say this during these times, as she continued to encourage me and speak directly into my spirit. "Baby, Momma needs you to get yourself together, okay? I know you're hurt; we're all hurt and devastated. But Durmond, I believe with every bit of Holy Ghost in me that your daddy gave God a *yes!* And because he gave God a, *yes*, I know I'm going to see him again one day. I know my husband made it in, and if YOU wanna see your Daddy again, baby, you're gonna have to give Him your *yes.*" She is such an inspiration.

I took it all in, but at the same time, truthfully, y'all, I wasn't trying to hear it. I was **broken** about my dad's death. I spent the last moments of my time in Rochester that week in tears. I was inside my parent's living room, hugging everyone goodbye as my family and I prepared to head back to Atlanta. I was extremely emotional because there were so many memories I had with my Pop in this house; From helping him mow the grass to snow blowing during the winter, sitting out in his truck listening to the '60s and '70s greatest hits, hearing him yell at me while trying to help him landscape the front yard. We had family fish frying to family reunions, listening to him give me advice on saving my money, listening to him and Shaft harmlessly argue about politics, boxing, women, or situations at work together. He was a hard-working man that loved his family. No one sat in his chair; he took great pride in how he thought and lived. He was and will forever be my **hero.** Rest In Power Pop, Mr. Thurman Harrell, Sr.

Chapter Twelve

When I returned to Atlanta, life seemed different. I was still somewhat in disbelief. However, I had to continue with life without my father. The first week was a serious reality check for me. I was used to calling him every day. I often would pick up my phone to dial his number, then crush my own heart knowing he was no longer here and wouldn't answer on the other end; it was torture.

I was back home in Georgia for eight days, still trying to cope with the inevitable. Exactly two weeks and one day after my dad was buried, I was home laying in bed, crying, tossing and turning, trying to speak to my dad's spirit. "I miss you, Pop. I don't know how I'm gonna do this without breaking down. I need you here, man."

At the moment, I felt like a lunatic. Why am I talking to him? Man, I'm going to sleep. So, I cried myself to sleep. When I finally drifted off, I had an enlightening dream, and I remember exactly how it went.

This was my dream: I was walking in a foggy forest. I was so disappointed and down. As I walked and cried, I came upon a long bench, and I sat down on it with my elbows on my knees and my face in my palms. My loud weeps were interrupted by what sounded like someone walking toward me. As I looked up with massive tears in my eyes, the footsteps stopped, and someone sat down on the bench with me. I looked up, and my father was looking at me with such a heavenly smile. I jumped up quickly, embraced him tightly, and cried aloud, "I miss you, man; I just wanted to hug you one time."

He said, "I miss you too, Durmond, and I know you're hurt, man, but you gotta keep going. You have so much more things to accomplish." I replied, "Yea, man, but I needed you to be here with me, Pop. I wanted you to be a part of the success I was having." He looked at me, smiled again, and said, "I am here with you. Every time you work in your yard, I'm there. When you kiss your children, I'm there. I'm always here, but Durmond, you gotta keep living your life."

As an unexplainable peace overtook me, I looked over and saw a beautiful little mixed girl about two or three years old with straight long black hair running and playing, smiling and laughing all by herself. There was such a distinctive glow about her. I looked at my dad with concern, "Man, why is that baby out here all by herself?"

Pop looked at me with his signature smirk and asked, "You don't know who that is?"

I chuckled, "Nah, man, who is that?"

He answered, "That's YOUR baby, Iyana."

She turned around and looked at me with the most gorgeous smile I've ever seen on a face, and I began to weep. That's when she ran up to him and hugged his leg, with her height peaking at about his knee. She couldn't stop smiling, still looking right at me.

I couldn't hold back the tears as I said, "I love y'all so much."

Pop replied, "We love you too, Durmond; now go live your life and everything you do, give it everything you got. We'll be here!"

I woke up with such a great peace over me. I got up, got dressed, and headed to work. While on the highway, in a place of authentic peace, with no music, no sound, just driving with the windows down, the breeze hit my face trying to process the dream. A still small voice whispered, "Are you going to give me a **Yes** now? Or is it still **okay?**"

It was so clear that I almost ran my car off the road. I had to gather myself as I pulled into a local plaza to gather my thoughts. I began to reflect on my dream, the pain, and **brokenness** I've endured, but most importantly, the words my mother had said, "If you want to see your dad again someday, you have to give God a **yes.**"

As I began to cry, I remember thinking, "Man, I'm so tired of crying." But I made up in my mind, "God, even though I'm hurting, even though I'm confused, even though I am **broken,** I'll eliminate my **okay**, and I'll say **YES** to you, your will, and your way."

I was tired of fronting. I was sick of perpetrating. I didn't want to pretend anymore. On the outside, it may have seemed like I had it all together, but inside, my soul was crying out for help. **Psalms 121:1-2 (KJV)** says, **"I will lift up mine eyes unto the hills, From whence cometh my help. My help cometh from the LORD, which made heaven and earth."**

Let me tell you, the moment I spoke it, I felt the entire weight of burden being lifted off my spirit. This was completely different from before, when I would declare "I'm delivered" and not know how I would feel the next day. I felt completely liberated, and it felt stupendous. I felt the chains break; I really felt the shackles loose. I began to ask God to forgive me for my wrongdoings, my indiscretions, and most importantly, my disobedience. I began to cry out to God and beg Him to please set me free; free in my mind and spirit, free in my walk and my talk. God, please *SET ME FREE*!!! **John 8:36 (KJV)** says, ***"If the Son, therefore, shall make you free, ye shall be free indeed."*** I promised Him that I would **commit** to **submit** and **persist** to **resist.**

I told the Lord if He would just deliver me fully, heal me completely, and put me back together again, I would run for Him like my life depended on it because, quite frankly, IT DID. God delivered me right there in that little plaza parking lot. I knew by the way my spirit shifted at that moment that the enemy was coming to retaliate. But I was determined that if he came at me *this time*, I was prepared to give it to God and allow Him to fight my battles. I knew that the Devil would dangle my past because that's the only weapon he had to try to bind me. Not this time, because God has blessed me to **let go** of everything from my past. So, when he does come in like a flood, I know that God will, according to **Isaiah 59:19 (KJV)**, ***"Lift up a standard against him."***

When monkeys are trapped, it's very strange and confusing how it happens. The first thing that the trappers do is place a heavy cage in the middle of the forest. The cage must be heavy enough so the monkey cannot lift the cage on its own. They also carve a mid-sized hole on the side of the cage. Then the trappers fill the cage with fruit such as kiwi, passion fruit, mangos, bananas, etc. Then, they sit back and wait. Sure, enough the monkeys would come ready to figure out a way to get to the fruit inside the cage.

The monkey would investigate and search the cage, trying to find a way in. It would suddenly see the carved hole on the side of the cage. The weird thing about this carved hole is that it's big enough for the monkey to fit its hand in to grasp the fruit of its desire. Now get this: the "trap" itself isn't the **cage** it's the **hole**. Why? Because the hole is big enough for the monkey's hand to fit in, but once the fruit was gripped, the hole wasn't big enough for the monkey's hand to pull back out. So now, the trap was set. The trappers would then just casually make their move toward the monkey with a metal club to strike it on its head, killing it instantly. The strange thing about this is that the monkey would see the trappers coming to kill it in most cases and has plenty of time to escape and live. But because some monkeys refused to **let go** of the fruit, they became victim to an easy trap.

In this life and this walk with God, the enemy will always try to find a way to trap us. How? With money, greed, fraudulence, sexual desires, and temptations. However, let us remember that **1 Corinthians 10:13 (KJV)** says, *"There hath no temptation taken you but such as is common to man: but God is faithful, who will not suffer you to be tempted above that ye are able; but will with the temptation also make a way to escape, that ye may be able to bear it."* We have a way to escape y'all. There is a way out.

The reason why we as saints of God find ourselves in so many traps it's because there are some things we just refuse to **let go** of, i.e., bitterness, anger, jealousy, envy, malice, and lack of forgiveness. These are things that God is trying to liberate us from. We worship, pray, praise, exalt and exhort, yet we find ourselves struggling to get delivered. We see the devil show its ugly face before it gets to us. Sometimes we see it coming and still can't shake the trap. Why? Because we just can't **LET IT GO** and be free. Not only that, but we also KNOW that the enemy desires to annihilate, extinguish and completely erase us and who we are.

John 10:10 (KJV) says, *"The thief cometh not, but for to steal, and to kill, and to destroy: I am come that they might have life, and that they might have it more abundantly."* He wants us to have life. He wants us to succeed. He wants us to be victorious. He doesn't want us to hold on to things that can hinder us, block us, or weigh us down. WE MUST LEARN TO **LET GO** and **LET GOD**. **Hebrews 12:1 (KJV)** says, *"Wherefore seeing we also are compassed about with such a great cloud of witnesses, let us lay aside every weight, and the sin which doth so easily beset us, and let us run with patience the race that is set before us."* When you are truly delivered, healed, and set free, you will begin to let things go that seemed impossible to let go of.

Slowly but surely, I began to let it all go. The hurt and pain that had followed me for years. The hatred towards the people who hurt me, the anger towards my ex, and those who ridiculed, lied on me and ran my name through the mud. The bitterness I had towards the Church that birthed who I was in God as a child. My smile was starting to become more authentic with time, the peace of God was flooding my spirit, and it felt amazing. It felt like as the days were going by, the layers of my past were peeled away from my spirit ONE BY ONE.

God was transforming me back to who I once was and who I used to be, and all I had to do was give Him a **yes,** as momma said. However, I still had a small issue to tackle with God's help. I had a preaching engagement for my cousin in Virginia, remember? I told her **okay!!**! Of course, I was in a different mindset when I told her *that;* but I still had to mount the platform and speak at this revival. I remember calling my sister Yolanda and saying, "Sis, I don't know if I can do this. It's been five years since I preached anywhere, and I don't know if I still 'got it,' man."

She began to minister to me and tell me, "No, bro, you definitely got this. We've been waiting for so long for you to come back. Just open your mouth and let Him speak for you."

My wife began to encourage me as well. When I met her, she didn't even know I was a preacher. The devil was trying to bury that part of me, and I was ok with that. So, Michele's approach of encouragement was a little bit different, "Babe, you have an opportunity to start back up in another region. You should be excited! I know I am. I can't wait to hear you for the first time."

I was so fearful y'all. I told her that it'd been a while since I'd preached, and the last time I was in it, my life was different. She began to assure me, "Baby, I promise you I will be there with you every step of the way. My support of you won't waiver, and my love for you won't change; YOU WERE BORN TO DO THIS. I know support means a lot to you. So, every time you mount the platform, I'll be front and center cheering you on!"

I never told her, but that was all I needed to hear from her to give me the confidence I needed to get through my "Re-Trial Sermon."

Leading up to the revival, I got a little annoyed because I was studying in His word, trying to figure out what I was going to say to God's people. I had NOTHING.

"Lord, why are you messing me up like this? I need your help. I don't wanna get up there and embarrass myself."

I would write a note here and a note there, then I would try to put them together with the scriptures and get stuck. "Man, come on, Lord, I need you to speak to me; the service is tomorrow night. Flyers have gone out locally and nationally on social media; please don't mess me up like this." That moment up to a few hours before service, I realized that I would have to walk by *faith* and not by *sight.*

Even when I mounted the platform to preach for the first time in five years, I had to deal with nervousness and anxiety. I felt my heartbeat in my throat, and my mind was racing all over the place. I looked into the light from the camera that was recording and saw flashes of my life; from sitting with my grandfather playing music to my first trial sermon message, to sitting in the homeless shelter, to playing the organ at church as an adult; the tears, the hurt, the pain, the anger, the hatred and bitterness, the confusion, Chad, my divorce, my baby's death, the cocaine addiction, the alcoholism, the strokes I suffered. To sum it all up, the **brokenness** I endured throughout my walk with and without God.

All these memories started to flood my head as I began to tear up and sweat profusely. But I remembered my liberation. I remembered how I was able to have more at this moment than I ever had in life itself, both spiritually and naturally. I have a beautiful family, who was there supporting me, a beautiful home, a great job, money in my pocket and bank account, and all my bills were paid. Knowing what I've gained and achieved from nothing to everything I've ever wanted with the help of God, His Son, and the Holy Ghost, I began to stand tall in that pulpit.

I genuinely smiled in **VICTORY,** knowing that God delivered and healed me from it ALL. **1 Samuel 30:8 (KJV)** says, *"And David enquired at the LORD saying, Shall I pursue after this troop? Shall I overtake them? And he answered him, Pursue: for thou shalt surely overtake them, and without fail recover all."*

So, the last flashback I had visioned before preaching was my father's face. He was looking at me with a smile. "Open your mouth and let Him speak for you," I heard his voice say.

When I opened my mouth to speak at that time, for the first time in a very long time, I felt so free and so liberated. I allowed the words from the scripture to flow from my lips with clarity, power, and most importantly, the anointing. Truthfully, I believe it was probably the most effective message I ever preached in all my years of preaching.

My point is this, if you give God your **yes,** in whatever you do for Him, especially from a place of freedom in your spirit, you will experience His power from a place that can not be explained, and He will do **Ephesians 3:20 (KJV),** *"exceedingly abundantly above all that we ask or think."* TO GOD BE ALL THE GLORY!

Chapter Thirteen

So, here's my take on everything you just read. At the beginning of this story, I was sharing the situation with the father and the daughter staring at the shattered, **broken** vase they had knocked off the table onto the floor from dancing and playing together. That father I was talking about was me, Durmond Lavell Glanton. The toddler-aged daughter was Itayvia. The vase that was **broken** on the floor was a special gift to me from my grandmother as a wedding gift back from my previous marriage. As I said initially, the value wasn't in the vase itself, but it was in the gift by its depth.

I sat there with Itayvia on my hip, sad, staring blankly at what I had just done while the music was still playing. While in deep thought, I felt awful, not knowing how I would explain to my grandmother the fact that I trashed the one thing I promised her I would keep with me forever. Obviously, that promise was now **broken** like the vase that was spread across the floor in many pieces.

Suddenly, out of the depths of my blank thoughts, a revelation enlightened me, which resurrected my excitement and energy. "I got an idea," I thought to myself.

I got Tay dressed, put her in the car seat in the car and headed towards the store to buy glue in an effort to save my vase. Silly, right? That's exactly what I thought as I walked up and down the store's aisles with a toddler on my hip, looking for the glue as though my life depended on it. "I must be outta my mind," I thought, *but* I was determined to make something happen.

As I got to the hardware aisle of the store, still holding the baby, I searched for the items until I came across a product called "Crazy Glue." The package stated that it was a "strong stick within minutes." Yes, this is the one I want. So, I bought two tubes of it, strapped Tay back in her car seat and headed back home.

When we got back to the house, the vase was still in pieces on the floor. I sat the baby on the couch and went and got the broom and dustpan to sweep up the **broken** pieces. I began to sweep up the pieces and place them on the glass table it once sat on. I kid you not; I counted nine pieces of the vase on my table before I started trying to put it back together piece by piece. I then began to apply the glue to certain parts of the vase, trying to match the pieces according to the cracks' measurements (*my spirit is leaping as I'm typing this*). I would apply the glue and connect the pieces, two by two separately, then let it sit for a few minutes until the stick was stable. I ended up with four connected pieces and a long piece of the vase on the table.

It was coming together, it seemed like, but it still looked **broken.** Carefully, after waiting a while, I repeated the process by applying the crazy glue and connecting the bigger pieces again two by two; within an hour and 30 minutes, all I had left was the long piece of the vase left on the table. This time, I waited a little longer to connect the final part of the vase. Let me tell you why. Because as I was connecting the vase piece by piece, there was glue seeping through and showing on the outside of the vase from the inside of the vase. So, as it was happening, I was taking a damp rag and wiping the visual glue that I saw on the outside. I wanted to make sure the vase was nice and dry yet still stable to stand.

So, I waited. When I finally applied the crazy glue to the final piece to connect to the rest of the vase, I wiped off the residue from the seeping glue on it and planned to let it sit for another 20 minutes.

I sat on the couch with Itayvia, and we both fell asleep just like that. When I woke up about an hour later, I saw the vase I had put back together sitting there. Itayvia was still sleeping. As I stared at this vessel, I began to tear up. Why? Because the vase looked twice as better as it did before it fell to the floor **broken** a couple of hours prior. The shine was different, and it looked like it was even standing stronger. It worked! It was fixed, and it didn't even look *broken.*

So, you may ask me, "Durmond, what does this story have to do with you or me?"

Here's the revelation God gave me, and I'm a living witness to this, you may be *broken,* but you're NOT beaten. You may be scattered, but NOT scorned. In pain, but NOT powerless. Distressed, but NOT defeated; terrorized, troubled, and tormented, but NOT tangled. Why? Because God will use all the "*crazy*" things that happen in your life as glue to somehow and some way, PUT YOU BACK TOGETHER AGAIN, and when He puts you back again, you will be BETTER than you were before the "break" took place. **Psalms 34:18 (KJV)** says, ***"The LORD is*** *nigh unto them that are of a broken heart; And saveth such as be of a contrite spirit."*

Never forget that the clay must go through a process in the potter's house and the potter's hands. It must be cut, scraped, smushed, smashed, shaped, and molded. The potter will NEVER put the clay on the shelf for display with unfinished pottery, but the process is necessary for it to be properly made fit for display. As the Bible informs us that we are *"Made in His image and likeness"* and *"Fearfully and Wonderfully made.* Please know that God will never put us on display for His Glory without going through the process. The good news in all this making is that the potter never takes his hands off the clay while he's shaping and molding it. The only time the potter takes his hands off the clay is when he puts the clay in the fire. However, I want to encourage you that even though the potter may take his hands off the clay, he keeps his eyes ON the clay. **Isaiah 43:2 (KJV)** says, ***"When thou passeth through the waters, I will be with thee; and through the rivers, they shall not overflow thee: when thou walkest through the fire, thou shalt not be burned; neither shall the flame kindle upon thee."*** The God that made the heavens and earth is Omnipresent. No matter where you are, what you do, or what you go through, God will always be there. I'm a living witness that He is a **"Very Present help in trouble."** **Psalm 46:1 (KJV)** THANK YOU, JESUS!

So, I sit here as a ball of emotions, looking back on everything I've gone through and experienced, be it good, not so good, bad, or even ugly. Walking with God now is different. I've made up my mind to walk with God no matter what. Has it been easy? Absolutely not. But I've learned that if walking with God no matter what was easy, then EVERYONE would do it. The "hard" is what makes it great and well worth it. I'm far from perfect, but I serve a perfect God with His grace and mercy. I rejoice, and I'm forever exceedingly glad because I could've been lost forever; my mind should've been gone, and I'm not saying it because it sounds cliché; I really should be in a psych ward on 24-hour watch after all I've gone through.

Isaiah 26:3 (KJV) says, *"Thou wilt keep him in perfect peace, whose mind is stayed on thee: because he trusteth in thee."* But can I be honest? Even when my mind wasn't on Jesus, God **kept** me. I'm so glad that God wouldn't let me die when some people didn't want me to live.

So, as I come before you, fully healed, fully delivered, and entirely set free, and NO

LONGER **broken,** and as an overcomer, I've realized many things by way of the Holy Ghost. My sinful ways and my pride kept me from an already unanimous victory. I spent so many years carrying bitterness, malice, and hatred in my heart. I wasted countless time pointing fingers at everyone else concerning my own problems.

The church, some of its members, my ex, and some family members all were on my "hit & hate" list when the truth was in the eye of the beholder. My spirit was vexed, I was jacked up, my pride was navigating my *process*, and all I had to do was say **"yes"** to God, His will, and His way. It was a rough road for me. A time in my life I will never forget. I experienced a lot of heartbreak and took some devastating losses, but knowing NOW that God had me. His perfect will makes me live a victorious life, completely encouraged and full of joy from a place that many others won't understand.

It's called living out **Philippians 4:7 (KJV)** **"Peace that surpasses all understanding."** I can truly announce to you that after all the things I've been through, I can live "in joy" and still "enjoy" my walk with the Lord, no longer **broken.** And because God allowed me to live through it, as His **Vase** *(vessel)* and through Him, I have elevated to another level. More joy, peace, a deeper love for Him, greater works, and greater anointing. It's the **Isaiah 10:27 (KJV),** *"Anointing that destroys yolks,"* right? God has anointed me in ways I never thought I could retain and retrieve. Even when I'm called to a platform to deliver His word, first and foremost, God never has to give me instructions again. Even if it sounds crazy, I bank on it and say *"yes"* to Him if He says it. However, when I'm called to a platform to preach, I feel His power, wisdom, and anointing flowing through me in a way I've never felt, and I realized this through my preaching.

When the woman anointed Jesus' feet with oil from the alabaster box **(Matthew 26:6-13) (KJV),** the value wasn't just in the oil but also in the vessel that carried the oil. Some vessels had to be *open* to pour the oil out, but some also had to be *broken* to get MORE oil. I understood that God allowed me to be *broken* to get more oil (anointing) out of my life. Although I was wrong, disobedient, rebellious, out of order, and out of control, He still saw fit to repair me by pouring more oil in me. You know, I have been enlightened. The things that I thought were the "hardest" things to do (which was to *commit to submitting*) was *actually* the "easiest" things to do.

For years, I thought I had so many enemies, but I finally realized that my biggest "enemy" was my "*inner me.*" The blindness of my own ignorance halted the things that God was trying to show me in the spirit. **2 Corinthians 4:4 (KJV)** says, ***"The god of this world has blinded the eyes of them that don't believe."*** I spent all those years looking for "the answer" when it was right in front of me the entire time. All that was needed was my belief. It doesn't matter how big your problems may be. The Giant BEFORE you will never be as big as the God that's IN you. Legendary comedian and actor Robin Williams once said, *"All it takes is one beautiful fake smile to hide an injured soul, and they will never notice how broken you really are."*

A lot of people look at my journey, they see my smile, my life, and my possessions, and they think my life was as close as can be too, perfect. They have no idea how many times I had to push through the pain. They're unaware of how often I had to smile to cover up my sinful situations. They see my accolades, awards, achievements, and accomplishments. They hear my on-air interviews, and they listen to others talk highly of me, but they have NO CLUE of the hell I had to endure, the forces of evil I had to fight, or the demons (both inner and outer) that I had to conquer to get here.

But this is my story; this is what it was, is, and will be for me. I am Durmond Lavell Glanton, and I was once a walking **broken vase**, hiding the inner cracks (within) behind my spirituality and my title. I was a lost soul, full of hate and bitterness. I was a lost mind, full of malice and pride. I was on my way to hell, thinking I was on the right track, but truthfully, I was on the wrong train. God allowed me to experience health defects, lose family members and close friends, depression, drug addiction, alcoholism, and suicidal battles. However, now I'm living obediently to God. I'm walking in my calling, walking in complete victory as I live my life now. I'm delivered, I'm healed, and I'm totally set free. No one must pay for the pain I've endured individually. What makes it all worth it is that I made a vow to God, both now and forever, that my answer will always be **yes.**

My brokenness played a huge role in my being processed by God. The individual things I experienced did not feel good, but I assure you that they ALL worked together for my good. When baking a cake (from scratch), you need flour, eggs, vanilla, yeast, baking powder, baking soda, salt, shortening, oil, butter, and a few other things. Now, tasting every ingredient individually doesn't taste good. Some of those ingredients are bad for you. But if you put them all together, the ending result will be a cake.

Let me tell you; I like the frosting on my cake too; however, what I am saying is this, the individual things I went through did not feel too pleasant. It caused heartache, heartbreak, tears, confusion, depression, affliction, addiction, and ultimately almost my life, but thanks be to God, who is rich in mercy, saw fit to give me another chance, and brought me out of a realm of darkness and put love, joy, and peace in my heart. On top of that (here's the "frosting"), He graced me with a renewed life to do this thing the right way. **Romans 8:28 (KJV)** says, ***"And we know that all things work together for good to them that love God, to them who are called according to his purpose."***

A few people expected me to fall, fail, and give up but are NOW confused, bitter, and envious because they feel as though I may be ***unqualified*** for the purpose in my life. To be truthful, I'm NOT qualified to be a pastor, NOT qualified to be a recording artist, NOT qualified to live in the house I live in, nor the vehicle I drive. But I serve a God who does not call the "qualified," but He qualifies the call. And when God calls you, no matter what you come against, be it by coincidence or consequence, God will fight for you while getting you back on the right track and the right train, fully liberated from it all. He will turn your "wounds" into "wisdom," He'll do it ALL for **HIS** glory.

Being **broken** is one of the hardest things to conquer, but my own **brokenness** is where I learned most of my lessons while gaining Godly wisdom. It is my desire to help as many people as I can to learn how to trust God while being **broken.** Trust Him, never doubt, know that He is a refuge, and I'm a living witness that He will bring you out stronger, wiser, smarter, BETTER, and NOT bitter.

GOD'S *MISSION...ACCOMPLISHED!*

About

Durmond Glanton

Every once in a while an exceptional and incredible talent impacts the gospel music industry and leaves a lasting impression. The anointed musical virtuoso **Durmond Glanton is** one of those rapidly expanding gospel artist who has done just that! When he sings he becomes a vessel through which the intent of worship and praise is fully recognized. Glanton brings to his listening *audience "worship and praise through song" with a personalized harmonic blend. What a supersized and engaging talent the* Lord has given to the industry!

Glanton was born on July 14, 1977. Nevertheless, he has encountered multiple series of attacks from the enemy on his life from conception. Yet God had a plan! In 2000, while attending a local revival in Rochester, NY, he received a **Word** from the Lord from Prophet Eric Cooper from Phoenix, Arizona. Prophet Cooper declared to him **"After the Storm, God is going to put your name in lights for the world to see."** Subsequently, he definitely encountered thunderous and tumultuous storms in his life! **He miraculously survived three strokes, beginning stage lung cancer, a minor heart attack, homelessness, drug addiction and suicidal battles. Today, however, if you were to ask him, "how were you able to go through all that, at such a young age and still survive?" His reply, simply would be, "when God is fighting for you, you can't lose." "People choose to be defeated, I choose to be *UNDEFEATED*with God on my side." He further encourages his audience "to not only praise God during the battle, but when the victory is won *REJOICE*." Accordingly, He is living the life and singing the praises!**

Glanton was a child prodigy! At the age of 4, he taught himself how to play the drums and he mastered the skill by the age of 9. Faithfully, he served as the church drummer until he was 22 years of age. His wonderment of music continued as he once again locked himself in a room and taught himself how to play the piano.

Please hear him in his finest hour on his current dual release single projects ***"Rejoice" and "Undefeated."*** These anointed releases offer a summary of Glanton's life story set to **music** which ends well! ***"Rejoice"*** features rhythmic agility and of course, the all-powerful toe tapping, hand clapping, praised infused impact. You can listen over and over to it when you're going through the storms of life. Remember, **Psalm 34:1 declares, "I will bless the Lord at all times. His Praise shall continually be in my mouth."** *Undefeated"* is his testament that he is a great example of overcoming all odds, and can **"rejoice"** knowing that only through Jesus Christ, we are **"undefeated."** These singles immediately establish a dialogue with the melody and lyrics with a personalized melodic/harmonic blend.

Besides, his extraordinary gifts and talents continue to revolutionize the gospel music industry coupled with inevitable proof of an even greater future.

Not only is he a skillful vocalist, creative music producer, and an anointed preacher. His talents transcend various creative art forms such as an innovative and accomplished songwriter, talented recording artist, choir director, vocal coach, music teacher, organist and drummer. He simultaneously projects his uncompromising vocal talents and gifts to an unprecedented

level of artistic achievement. Simply stated he excels in the excellent!

Glanton is currently serving as an accomplished organist at the Bethlehem Temple Church of a New Beginning in the Atlanta, GA area. His foremost goals in Kingdom work and in life is changing the world "One song at a time." Glanton's plan for the faith community is to give back to the less fortunate churches in their music departments by assisting them to develop strong Bible based musicians for Ministry.

A quick glance of his exceptional accomplishments is quite impressive. **Glanton has shared the stage with world renowned artists such as: Tye Tribbett, The Clark Sisters, Bobby Jones and Keith Wonderboy Johnson.**

Accordingly, Durmond Glanton cordially invites you to share his journey as you *"Rejoice"* and remain "Undefeated." You will be glad you did!

www.ingramcontent.com/pod-product-compliance
Lightning Source LLC
Chambersburg PA
CBHW070719130626
46553CB00005B/2057